YA HA TINDA

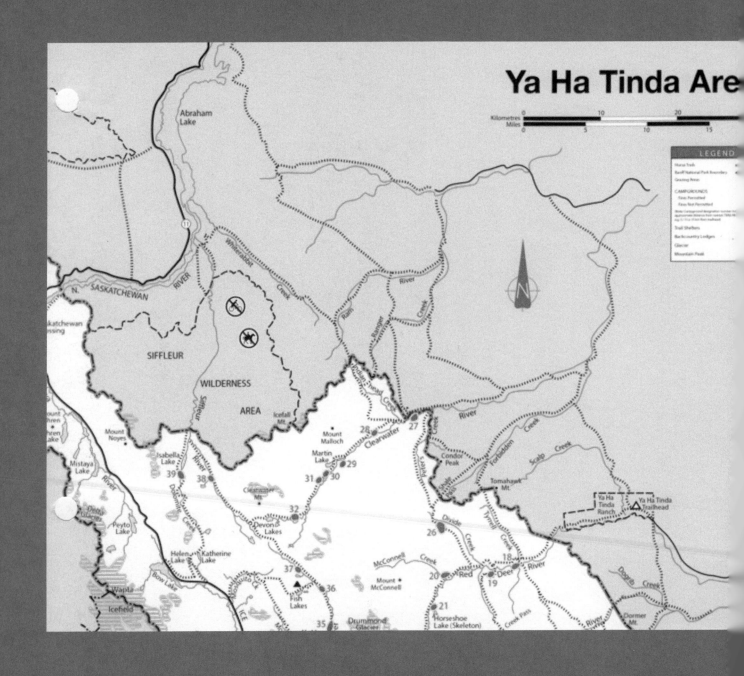

Ya Ha Tinda Area

KATHY CALVERT

YA HA TINDA

A Home Place

Celebrating 100 Years of the Canadian Government's Only Working Horse Ranch

RMB

To the men and women of the National Park Service who helped make the Ya Ha Tinda a successful working horse ranch for over a century,

and

To those who lived and worked on the Ya Ha Tinda providing years of devoted stewardship to the land and the horses.

CONTENTS

Foreword   9

Chapter 1: Discovery   13

Chapter 2: The Golden Years   37

Chapter 3: An Uncertain Future   65

Chapter 4: Some Degree of Settlement   85

Chapter 5: Resolution to an Elusive Future   119

Chapter 6: The Shifting Scene   147

Acknowledgements   177

Donors   179

Ya Ha Tinda Bound   181

Notes   183

FOREWORD

It was my great privilege in the '60s and '70s, and for half of 1988, to work as a national park warden in the Rocky Mountains, just about the best job in the world on most days. The warden service was, in part, a cavalry outfit, so it was my good fortune, as a lifelong student of western history, to be required to work on horseback, learning the skills under the tutelage of some old-timers for patrolling with saddle and pack horses in the backcountry of Yoho, Banff and Jasper national parks.

In those days, always short-handed it seems, wardens often travelled alone from 18 to 24 days at a stretch. The main form of communication in Jasper was a No. 9 telephone wire strung from pole to pole and from tree to tree throughout the district. This was our line to the outer world in case of emergencies such as wildfires, bear incidents, lost backpackers or climbing accidents. Woe betide the warden whose phone line was not in service when Chief Park Warden Mickey McGuire called. Hauling all the equipment required to maintain hiking trails and that telephone line, which everything in nature from wandering moose to spring avalanches conspired against, required us to travel with anywhere from one to five pack horses. It took one horse just to haul the wire, insulators and pole-climbing harness, another to haul the chainsaw, fuel and hand tools, another to haul the grub and camping supplies, and perhaps two others laden with everything from oats to hay bales to asphalt shingles and paint for the line cabins. To add to the challenges, one of the horses might be a colt, sometimes a hot-blooded thoroughbred that had been trained for riding and packing on the Ya Ha Tinda, the government horse ranch, and was now finishing its schooling out in the bush.

This experience put us directly in the tradition of lives lived in these mountains by the equestrian tribes of pre-contact times, notably the Ktunaxa (Kootenay), Nakoda (Stoney) and the Piikani (Peigan) people and the old-time surveyors, outfitters, rangers and park wardens who followed in their hoofprints. Though a warden might travel solo, the horses certainly kept him company, alternately amusing and exasperating with their antics as they jockeyed for the lead position on narrow mountain trails. At night, the distant sound of a battered Swiss bell, hung around an older mare's neck as she grazed in the meadow near the line cabin or tent, was a reassuring lullaby to the ear. These were working horses, not pets, and they worked with me, not for me, showing me around the districts they had worked in during the years before I had arrived on the scene.

As backcountry wardens, the backcountry district was the focus of our work and our concern, but the heart and soul of the operation (and the subject of this book) was the Ya Ha Tinda ranch located west of Sundre, Alberta, on the east boundary of Banff National Park. This was the wintering range for most of the park cavvy. Since I was stationed for a time at Scotch Camp, on the Red Deer River, I often circled out onto provincial land down the Red or Panther rivers to try and catch a poacher or two sneaking over the Banff park boundary line to score a trophy ram. These autumn patrols might take me by the ranch, where ranch staff would invite a guy to "fall off and stay awhile" for a hot coffee, or a warm bunk if the hour was late. It was a pleasure to spend a night in front of the wood stove listening to foreman Slim Haugen and the other cowboys spin yarns of wild days in the saddle. Mostly the talk was of horses, horses long dead and gone or tributes to likely colts that would be up for bids in the spring. The talk might turn to famous bronc riders, or the doings of visiting biologists and

their fascination with elk poop, or the comings and goings of the local pack of grey wolves. If the western branch of the park warden service had a spiritual nexus, then its guardian angels were at play around that stove while snowflakes piled up on the windowpanes.

The warden service has not fared well in recent years, as you will learn in this book. In fact, it was effectively gutted in 2008, after a hundred years of devotion to the cause of national parks, and reduced to a ghost of itself. But that's another story. As you will learn here, the Ya Ha Tinda weathered that storm. It has survived many political attempts on its life, thanks to an informed and attentive public and some dedicated civil servants, and it has evolved to serve both provincial and federal governments, as well as a rich habitat for wildlife, as an equestrian training centre, a centre for biological, environmental and archaeological research and as a great natural resource for the thousands of people who come to camp, hike and ride its trails, or to access the backcountry of Banff National Park. The Ya Ha Tinda is a vibrant part of the ranching history of Alberta, a heritage that is in dwindling supply these days. It's always been a home on the range, and now it has also become a home where the buffalo roam.

I for one look forward to seeing the ranch

continue in its western heritage traditions on into the next century. May it always be there, to be discovered by many new generations of Canadians who need a place where they can slow their lives down for a little while, and step or ride back into the past on ancient trails that will lead them back again, renewed, into the future.

—Sid Marty, May 2017

Welcome gate to the the Ya Ha Tinda.

CHAPTER 1
DISCOVERY

An almost mythical land which lay back in the mountains.
—Pat Brewster, *Weathered Wood: Anecdotes and History of the Banff-Sunshine Area*

Deep within the east slopes of the Rockies just west of Sundre, Alberta, lies a high open grassland surrounded by stunning protective mountains first named Ya Ha Tinda by the Stoney people, meaning "Mountain Prairie."[1] This broad rolling plateau, dominated by rich fescue grass, is blessed with a mild climate and rarely sees passing storms, which are deflected by the high protective ridges. The winter Chinook winds funnel down the Red Deer River, keeping the land open and snow-free most of the year.

Anyone who visits the Ya Ha Tinda and experiences first-hand the unique beauty of these grasslands, embraced by the sheltering mountains and green rolling hills, knows why people have been drawn here over the centuries. If they are lucky that day, they may encounter some of the abundant wildlife that lives in this rich montane environment. If so, they may wonder who the first people were to find this valley and how long ago that was.

One theory is that early prehistoric peoples entered the North American continent from Asia across the Bering Strait land bridge before rising seas submerged it. From there, they may have travelled through an ice-free corridor along the eastern slopes of the Rocky Mountains to colonize the habitable lands in the northwest. Other seafaring people have left evidence of boating down the west coast as far as California, from where they could move northward as the icefields retreated.[2] Wherever they came from, the archaeological record shows very early human habitation at the Ya Ha Tinda after the great glaciers began to recede. P.D. Francis, one of the first archeologists to study the Ya Ha Tinda, states, "The cultural-historic

Horse racing at Morley Alberta.

records in the area hold evidence of multiple human occupations that may extend back 10,000 years and thus, have a bearing upon the compelling archaeological question about the initial peopling of North America."[3]

The hunter-gatherer culture of prehistoric peoples in North America depended on the presence of big game in sufficient quantities to provide a staple food supply. During the early prehistoric period to the middle prehistoric period (5500–3000 BC), there is archaeological evidence to show that bison (more commonly called buffalo) migrated through this high prairie, probably drawing these people here in search of game. Certainly, prehistoric sites have been found on the ranch. Luigi Morgantini reports, "Initial analysis of the sites suggested that over the centuries the area was repeatedly occupied by prehistoric culture groups with cultural relationships with the Northern Plains and possibly with tribes from the interior of British Columbia."[4] A major archaeological site at the eastern edge of the ranch shows evidence of thousands of years of bison hunting – certainly the grasslands are pitted by some of the highest densities of "buffalo wallows" in the Rocky Mountains.[5] In these dish-like dips in the soil, often several metres across, the great beasts once rolled and threw up billowing clouds of dust during the summer mating

season. The small pit house villages found further up the Red Deer Valley indicate that the Salish people from the west coast also crossed the mountains to hunt buffalo here.

The precise travels of First Peoples and animals from the Ya Ha Tinda across the eastern slopes of the Canadian Rockies over the last 3,000 years has too little archaeological evidence to state where all the migratory routes went or where they settled for any length of time. Though Morgantini found scant information about the life of the early dwellers on the ranch, commenting, "Little is known of the Ya Ha Tinda prior to 1800," there is enough to give us a tantalizing glimpse of that time.[6] As with any people's history, there are discrepancies, particularly between oral lore and recorded observations of early explorers. Nonetheless, it is possible to form a plausible outline of early Aboriginal movement and habitation throughout and around the Ya Ha Tinda prior to the appearance of the first European explorers. Of these, the Stoney people were the most recent First Nations to call the Ya Ha Tinda home within the parameters of a transitory lifestyle. There is much speculation as to how they came by the name "Stoney." It has been mentioned that the name "Stoney" was derived from placing hot rocks in water-filled baskets to boil their food. However, that was a common practice among many First Nations people. Pat Brewster wrote of another source of this name. He had heard that "they were called the Stone or Rock Indians by the Blackfoot (Luxton) which eventually mutated into the name 'Stoney.'"[7]

The Stoney–Nakoda bands were essentially extended families (or bands) that inhabited the more mountainous areas of the Rocky Mountains from the headwaters of the Athabasca River in the north to Chief Mountain in Montana just south of the Canadian border. Here they were known as Rocky Mountain Sioux. Their oral tradition claims they lived here "from time immemorial," but the first recorded story (by the early Jesuits) indicates they originated from the Dakota/Lakota Nation that is now North and South Dakota in the United States.[8]

The early fur trade was ever pushing west with the support of the Cree, and it seems likely many of the extended families of the Dakota joined them in their western migration.[9] Several things would have enticed them on this journey. As the white traders brought profit, they also brought guns, liquor and disease. Tribal warfare escalated and aggressive bands began driving out the more peaceable factions. As early as 1690, Henry Kelsey, a fur trader working for the Hudson's Bay Company, travelled with the Stoney–Assiniboine up to the Saskatchewan River. Anthony Henday, in 1754, possibly the first European to see the Canadian Rockies, found several Stoney–Assiniboine camps in Alberta (probably around Innisfail, 18 miles south of the Red Deer River). It seems that once the Stoney reached the mountains, they continued to expand south, always keeping well within the mountains and away from the warlike Blackfoot tribes. Historical researcher Raoul Anderson cites other researchers who hold "that the Assiniboine split off into two westward moving branches after their separation from the (Yanktonai) Dakota sometime prior to the 17th century. One branch moved northwest along the edge of the plains keeping close contact with the Cree. A southern branch later moved to Montana where they sought shelter in the mountains in the west."[10]

The approximate dates of the Stoneys' arrival and settlement of the eastern slopes of the Rockies varies, depending on the source and location. Ted Binnema and Melanie Niemi, in their study of the exclusion of First Nations from national parks, wrote, "The Siouan-speaking Stoney (Nakoda) probably arrived in historic times – almost certainly after 1790, and perhaps not until the mid-1800's – but they knew the place well by 1870. Surveyors and explorers of the late nineteenth century typically turned to Stoney guides, and as a result many landforms in Banff National Park are still known by their Stoney names."[11]

Throughout that time, the Stoney developed their camps, trading routes and hunting grounds. But they certainly did not have "time immemorial" to do so, as by the early 1900s their way of life had disappeared when they were confined to the reservations they now live on – a short span of time in relative history. Though the buffalo were disappearing rapidly, elk and deer were plentiful. Bighorn sheep were also abundant on the open south-facing slopes. Judging by the many tipi rings found on the Ya Ha Tinda, the Stoneys and previous occupants spent considerable time camped there year-round, finding it especially good for winter camps with its mild climate.

Hunter-gatherer societies like the Stoneys were also, by necessity, nomadic. They were a sociable people and travelled widely, not only for hunting but to trade as well. No doubt many ceremonies and celebrations accompanied their meetings with other tribes of the Rockies, providing an opportunity to visit extended family members. Morgantini, in reference to the Ya Ha Tinda and the surrounding area, states, "Numerous well-traveled trails along the East Slopes attest to ancient use of the region."[12] The Stoneys constantly travelled north and south of the Bow River valley, but particularly

between Morley, northwest of Calgary, and the Kootenay Plains on the Saskatchewan River. This made for frequent visits to the Ya Ha Tinda grasslands, where they would stay for extended periods.

Norman Luxton, an early resident of Banff, was intrigued by the Stoneys and came to know many of them first-hand. He speculated that the Ya Ha Tinda was a perfect location for them because it supplied food, graze, shelter and abundant water. More importantly, however, there was only one entrance to the upper Red Deer from the plains, through a narrow gorge-like valley. It provided additional protection from the Cree, Blackfoot and, occasionally, the Sarcee.[13]

By the time the Stoneys settled along the foothills and into the mountains, they had separated into a number of small bands. The Bearspaw band was closer to the Blackfoot in lifestyle and temperament, being the most warlike of the bands. They lived a semi-plains existence ranging from the foothills of Crowsnest Pass to the Bow River valley, and relied heavily on buffalo for a main food source. The Chiniki band lived north of the Bow River and into the Bow Valley, where they sought out beaver and local game but made occasional forays east onto the plains for buffalo. The Goodstoney band, the most peaceful and shy people of the three

bands, resided much deeper in the foothills and mountains, with their main base being the Kootenay Plains on the North Saskatchewan River. The Goodstoney band subsisted almost entirely as a woodland people. Though separated by differences in culture and space, these bands often camped and hunted together, maintaining ties, probably through marriage.[14]

The Stoneys' short-lived tenure on the Ya Ha Tinda was lost soon after the Canadian Pacific Railway (CPR) was completed in 1885, bringing about the creation of Rocky Mountains

National Park (now Banff National Park). With or without the creation of the park, the Stoneys were having a difficult time living anywhere in the West by the late 1800s. Like the buffalo, they, too, were fading from the landscape. The sudden decline of Aboriginal people in western Canada began with the loss of the buffalo that began to dwindle dramatically prior to the 1880s. By 1880, the number of Stoneys was perilously low. This sad part of Alberta's history (and the West in general) is documented in the book, *Alberta in the 20th Century*. In their traditional eastern slope homelands, the First Nations had thrived, and "few would have believed that in the next two decades, this world was to collapse into squalor."[15] The Stoneys, who so assiduously avoided famine and disease by living in the secluded slopes of the Rockies, were no longer protected from these devastating forces. Sickness, starvation and death crashed down on them suddenly, hastened by the loss of their traditional hunting grounds with the creation of Rocky Mountains National Park.

The Stoneys' new home reservation was established at Morley, just east of Banff National Park. Binnema and Niemi write, "The Methodist mission at Morleyville [Morley] was established in 1873, before its residents signed the treaty. Parts of their reserve, surveyed in 1879, were suitable for grazing, but none was promising agricultural land." Though the reserve was established for the Stoneys, initially, not many of them stayed on it, preferring to live and hunt where they always had. Even the Indian agents encouraged them to hunt on the eastern slopes during the early 1880s, when buffalo was scarce and farming or cattle provided little food. But it was the arrival of the CPR that radically changed their lives. "Most obviously, the CPR brought rapid environmental change. Wildfires – caused by cinders from locomotives or by careless newcomers and visitors that arrived with the railway, depleted the game." Also, according to W.F. Whitcher, who was quoted by Binnema and Niemi, in 1886, "skin-hunters, dynamiters and netters, with Indians, wolves and foxes, have committed sad havoc." Already, in 1886, the Department of Indian Affairs annual report noted, "The hunt of these Indians for fur-bearing animals and game has not been attended with the same success since the railway was built. The latter had the effect of driving the animals to much more distant parts ... relief has had at times been sent by the Department to the hunters to enable them to return to their reserve."[16]

It took time for the Stoneys to accept living on the reserve, and for years they continued to hunt in the mountains, even after the creation of the park. But, inevitably, the old knowledge and traditions were lost. The trails connecting them to the Kootenay Plains on the Saskatchewan and Athabasca rivers farther north were gradually forgotten. Fading, too, were the trails to the Eden Valley and the southern part of their earlier range. It remained for the cowboys and archaeologists to rediscover remnants of these ancient trails.

The discovery of hot springs, surrounded by the splendours of the mountains, became the doorway to the vision of creating Canada's first national park. The initial thought was that the hot springs, which led to the creation of the small town of Banff, would provide a magnet for the flocks of affluent easterners looking for adventure. The fuss over the hot springs prompted Ottawa to send out a Dominion land agent to see if a land claim for the springs was worth considering. What he and fellow visitor, P. Mitchell, a former Conservative MP, found may have surprised them. Mitchell reported to Prime Minister John A. Macdonald that the springs and natural beauty surrounding it had considerable value. He estimated the value to be "at least half a million of dollars."[17] Rather than grant exclusive rights to Frank McCabe and William McCardell (the men who actually found the hidden cave that sourced the hot springs), the government decided to keep it. In 1887, an order-in-council created Canada's first national park, with the uninspired name of Rocky Mountains National Park. But, initially, the ten acres of land surrounding the Banff townsite and the hot pools received little protection from the declaration. The inevitable happened and, within two years after the railway's completion, the depredation of the wildlife and forests became alarming. The obvious greed forced the federal government to create an actual national park with boundaries that endeavoured to protect the resources and manage the conservation of a much larger park. The Canadian government may have been influenced to incorporate these lofty, rather remote ideas after the United States created the first national park in the world at Yellowstone. Whatever led to these ideas, Rocky Mountains National Park was quickly expanded to include the Ya Ha Tinda as early as 1885, even before the order-in-council was passed.[18]

In 1887, George Stewart, the first superintendent appointed to Banff, was overwhelmed by the extent of his responsibilities in protecting the wildlife (of which he was a proponent). The first regulations included a clause that would prohibit visitors from killing or injuring any wild animals, with the exception of carnivores. Weapons were also prohibited to park visitors. He also advocated for "game guardians" to enforce the new regulations. The Stoneys, now

forbidden to hunt in their traditional hunting grounds, created fewer problems than the local white population. It took some time to re-educate the white usurpers to respect the new rules. Stewart finally obtained some assistance when he was able to hire John Connor in 1889 as the first forest ranger whose principal job was to protect the park from fire hazards. His secondary but equally important job was to enforce the firearms regulations. John Connor was a born environmentalist, and those who poached or set fires vexed him to no end. He

found the locals to be very lax in their attitude toward gun control, constantly finding "people carrying rifles around, and banging them off whenever they like."[19]

Real change began in the early 1900s when Howard Douglas was brought in to replace Stewart as superintendent of the park. Douglas was an adamant environmentalist and fought vigorously for the protection of the park. When the park was expanded in 1902 to encompass realms of land he could barely fathom, let alone see, he knew he would need a substantial law enforcement body to protect these far-flung borders.[20] He would need all the help he could get when Alberta officially became a province in 1905, with its own unclear ideas of jurisdiction and guardianship. Thus began the see-saw struggles of the Ya Ha Tinda to remain a federal government ranch, as the province and the federal government began their 100-year battle over control of this remote area.

Conflict over jurisdiction began almost immediately in 1907, when the Alberta government took it upon itself to enforce the game regulations in Rocky Mountains National Park, and even went as far as to post "no hunting" cloth notices on the (as yet) unsurveyed boundaries. This astonished and affronted Douglas, who viewed the park as federal land completely under his jurisdiction. Douglas had his own game warden to enforce no hunting in the park and wondered if the province had plans to send its own men in. Douglas made Ottawa aware he had his own chief game warden (Philip A. Moore) to enforce the firearms regulations and also enforce what he continued to view as federal regulations.[21]

Unfortunately, one of the issues not addressed immediately by either government was the question of grazing rights. Though Douglas firmly believed that private grazing had no place in a federal park, the province had no problem with grazing on Crown land. The new provincial government was particularly sensitive to the needs of ranchers. Though the decision to grant the lease remained with the federal government, the sympathy of the province for ranchers created a tailor-made opportunity for one of early western Canada's most famous entrepreneurial families: the Brewsters.

Thus, the written history of the Ya Ha Tinda as a ranch begins with the Brewsters. By the mid-1880s, John Brewster was looking for business opportunities after settling in Banff with his wife and their seven children. John heard rumours of a mountain-enclosed prairie to the north, interestingly enough from a Stoney man who told him of "this mythical land."[22] His name was William Twin and he had lived to see the glory and the decimation of his people. He was born in 1847 when the land to the First Nations people was considered free to all. William was best described by the Reverend Mr. Staley, who spoke at his funeral at the Stoney Indian Reserve where he is buried beside his twin brother Joshua, "from whom he was inseparable in life." Both men lived until they were 97, dying only a few months apart. Mr. Staley eulogized William's character as "simple and sincere," living a life of humility and practical Christian virtues.[23] He accepted but was puzzled by the concept that any individual could own the land. It was strange to a man who had lived his life freely and was probably surprised the Brewsters wanted to claim the Ya Ha Tinda. The fact that Canada as a whole had been claimed by a government as far away as England must have seemed ludicrous to him.

Twin was leader of the Wildman band that wintered on the Kootenay Plains on the Saskatchewan River well into the mountains. As a youth, he followed the old trails up the Siffleur River, over Pipestone Pass and down to Lake Louise (then called Laggan). From there they would travel down the Bow Valley to Banff. All of these places were well known to

William Twin.

the Stoneys, who often met near Banff to trade with the Kootenai tribes from British Columbia and other tribes from the prairies. By the late 1880s, however, things had changed dramatically in the West and Banff was now a town owned by white people. Yet the Stoneys were peaceable by nature, and flexible as well. Young William was energetic and opportunistic. John Brewster's business started by running a dairy farm near the town to supply the CPR train passengers, crews, its new hotel (Banff Springs) and the growing residential population with dairy products. Brewster was always in need of a good hand and was happy to hire the young Twin, as he was called. A new future was opening up for the young Twin that contrasted dramatically with his early years, but he embraced it, along with his growing friendship with John Brewster. John soon had William helping him with the hay harvests, for which he would return each summer from the Kootenay Plains. When John died, William's ties to the Brewster family remained. He proclaimed to John's children, "John gone. God take him. Now me your father."[24]

William seemed especially close to John's son Jim, who he taught to hunt and speak Cree. He also brought him to Mystic Lake, probably the first white man to lay eyes on the beautiful body of water below Mystic Pass that teemed with fish. William seemed intent on his friend John Brewster becoming acquainted with the country that was his former heritage and cajoled him into further explorations. Pat Brewster, the youngest son of John and Bella, wrote, "William's persuasive conversation with my father about an almost mythical land, which lay back in the mountains about 3 days journey north of Banff finally lead [sic] to the trip [to] the beautiful prairie" surrounded by its protective horseshoe of mountains.[25] Though the origin of the name "Ya Ha Tinda" remains in dispute (and probably always will be), William called it "Mountain Prairie" in English. It seemed appropriate to Jim Brewster. Not only that but he immediately perceived the value of this highland oasis. It spawned acres of the precious rough fescue grass, richly watered by numerous streams, a place ideal for horses. He trusted William when he said it also had mild winters blessed by warm Chinook winds that kept the land free of snow most of the year round. With the abundance of workers showing up in Banff looking for employment, it would not be much of a task to clear the old travelling trails over Snow Creek Summit and down the Cascade River to Banff. The Brewsters were expanding into other ventures at an alarming rate. Their burgeoning backcountry outfitting business would need a good supply of

well-wintered horses. Land available for wintering horses was rapidly being bought up and was becoming expensive as well. This made the untouched Ya Ha Tinda plains a valuable investment, but it would require some negotiation to acquire them. Though it was officially on federal land, the Province of Alberta fought this jurisdiction from the beginning. The Ya Ha Tinda ranch was born in a climate of political controversy, greed and misunderstanding before it ever became a horse ranch for the federal government.

With nothing to lose, the Brewsters applied to Douglas for a grazing lease in 1904.[26] Douglas at first refused, saying it was incompatible with the park, but the Brewsters persisted and applied again the following year. This resulted in them obtaining a lease at the junction of the Panther and Red Deer rivers. It was not where they really wanted to be, as the prime land was just west of the confluence of Scalp Creek and the Red Deer River 18 miles upstream. They took advantage of the fact that the park really did not know the country and soon established a cabin there before actually obtaining the lease. By 1907, they re-established the ranch where the Ya Ha Tinda ranch now exists and soon carved out a route over Snow Creek Summit to Banff. They took little time in running both cattle and horses in the open meadows. This trip from Banff to what was then called the Brewster Ranch took three days, and pack trains with supplies travelled through there regularly during the summer months.

Frank Sibbald, brother to Howard Sibbald, became the first ranch manager in 1907. It is interesting that the Brewsters hired Frank to oversee the ranch, as his brother Howard would soon become an opponent of their continued tenure in the park. That was, of course, after he became the first chief park warden in Canada and the architect of the future National Park Warden Service. Howard previously worked as an Indian agent in 1902 at the Morley Indian Reserve just east of present-day Banff National Park. He was aware of the plight the Stoney faced, being removed from their hunting grounds with the creation of the park, but, like most white men at the time, he felt they would benefit in the long run. He wrote, "The Stoney took the enlargement of the Banff National Park very hard … a hard blow to some of the old Siouan-speaking Nakoda-Stoney hunters …

who have hunted over this ground all their lives."[27]

The Stoneys were hurting and felt their cause was being ignored by the government. In desperation, they addressed their complaints in a letter written in 1907 to the new provincial government:

> *They tell us that we must not hunt the goat and sheep in the mountains … that we must not kill more than one moose, one caribou, one deer and that we must pay $2.50 before we can hunt. Now, when we made a treaty with your chiefs, we understood that there would always be wild animals in the forest and the mountains. But the white men come every year, more and more, and our hunting grounds are covered with the houses and fences of white men. We are poor people. We do not know how to get money as white men do … Look kindly upon us, oh white chiefs. Let us still hunt the game in the fall as our fathers did. We work hard and make all the money we can, and we buy what the white men eat, but sweeter to us than all, is the flesh of the wild animals…. Give us freedom to go into the mountains and the forests to look for meat of the wild animals, and the birds, when our children ask for it.*[28]

It was very difficult for the Stoneys, who had

so little time to adjust to this sudden change in their lives. However, Douglas was already lamenting the loss of animals in the park as early as 1903. When he became superintendent, he had been impressed by the abundance of moose, elk, sheep, goats and deer. He was even happy to see a healthy population of black bear. But, in an early report to Ottawa, Douglas voiced serious concern that some of these species had totally disappeared. He must have been referring to the elk that were no longer being seen in the mountains and plains of Alberta. A combination of severe winters and overhunting by both white men and Aboriginal people had decimated the population, and they would not return until they were reintroduced many years later. He unconditionally blamed the depletion on the Stoneys' hunting skills: "The Stoney Indians are primarily responsible for this condition of affairs. They are very keen hunters, and have always been, and they are the only Indians who hunt in this section of the mountains. For years, from their reserve, they have systematically driven the valleys and hills and slaughtered the game. Their lodges are full of wild skins and meat."[29] He rails on in this manner, not really acknowledging that much of this hunting ground was lost to the Stoneys when the park boundaries were set.

Some of the blame for poaching can be laid at the feet of the Brewster cowboys who took their share of the game. Whether Douglas unfairly used the Stoneys as a scapegoat (rather than implicate the richer, more politically connected, Brewsters) to hire more game guardians, he did obtain three more men. He felt unfailingly that enforcement was badly needed. He concluded his report by forcefully stating, "Let the line be drawn now; if we wait longer, the game will be gone."[30]

When Douglas was free to hire more men, he also hired Howard Sibbald, who he appointed chief fire and game warden of the Fire and Game Warden Service. Sibbald took this job seriously, which would become his life work for which he is recognized today. The new job had two principal concerns: fire control and game protection. In this endeavour, his attention soon focused on the activities of the Brewster cowboys. Interestingly enough, just as Douglas was gaining ground in protecting the new park, the eastern boundaries were reduced in 1911 by the passage of the Dominion Forest Reserve and Parks Act. It was a huge loss of territory to the province that included the Ya Ha Tinda ranch. Historian Jim Taylor states, "The Act reduced much of the undeveloped areas of the park by designating undeveloped timbered areas as Dominion Forest Reserves. At the same time, the Act provided for the two centralized management structures to look after parks and forest reserves. Dominion Parks were managed by the Parks Branch and forest reserves by the Forest Branch of the Department of the Interior."[31]

Douglas was appalled by the loss of this land, which he considered "suicidal policy,"[32] but he was fortunate in having considerable support in Ottawa with the inauspicious appointment of J.B. Harkin as commissioner of the newly formed Dominion Parks Branch in 1911. Harkin was young at the age of 36 for this appointment, but it would be one that would last, to the betterment of all Canadian national parks. He was an enlightened Christian thinker who saw "the wilderness as the ultimate expression of God's handiwork." His main concern was the protection of game. The restoration of the old boundaries became one of his priorities. Though new to the job, he immediately recoiled from a clause in the act that was put in to "satisfy the mining and lumbering interests of the day."[33]

The Dominion forests were overseen by forest rangers whose principal job was to monitor resource extraction of trees, though, at the time, Rocky Mountains National Park was given to understand that wildlife would also be protected. The forest rangers, however, were mainly loggers and not trained in any law

Commissioner J.B. (Bunny) Harkin, appointed first Dominion Parks Branch Commissioner in 1911. Under his leadership the number of parks was tripled to eighteen by 1932.

COURTESY WHYTE MUSEUM OF THE CANADIAN ROCKIES.

enforcement capacity. Despite this, they were given the authority to enforce the Alberta wildlife regulations that allowed hunting on the forest reserves.

The province was supposed to supply these men but did little to hire the necessary staff. In the end, it was the national park game guardians under Sibbald who undertook patrolling the forest reserves for game infractions (for the Alberta government). It was an untenable situation. Forestry Branch Commissioner R.H. Campbell wanted to see the Dominion forest reserves expanded, as did the head of Parks

Branch, J.B. Harkin, but for different reasons. It was classic empire building for control over a considerable amount of land. Exactly who had authority over federal land (and for what) became very murky during the next several years.

The Brewsters were not slow to capitalize on the change in jurisdiction and the confusion that seemed to be rampant throughout the different departments of both governments. Their lease was located right in the middle of prime sheep habitat, from which they could base lucrative hunting expeditions. They were also fairly free in ignoring national park boundaries, which they travelled through to access the ranch from Banff townsite.

This infuriated Howard Sibbald, who repeatedly stated, "99% of the poaching [by Brewster men] has been done by these people under the guise of coming to and from the ranch."[34] This frustration deepened Howard's determination to establish a valid law enforcement body, with enough men to be present when these offences were occurring. To this end, he worked tirelessly, establishing trails accessing the eastern boundary of the park, dotted with well-placed cabins where the men could live for long stretches and monitor the activities of anyone using the park. Sibbald travelled extensively himself, and probably knew the Ya Ha Tinda area well enough to know where problem areas existed.

Howard Sibbald was a unique and determined man who lived by one law: protect the park. Sid Marty refers to it as "Sibbald's Law," which "was as hard to maintain as it was easy to state."[35] Though game protection was a priority, his main fear was a repeat of the devastating fires that were a significant factor in the history of settlement of the Rockies, both in Canada and the United States. One of the most devastating fire seasons occurred in 1910, shortly after Howard became a fire chief for the park. This fire started in the Cascade Mountains in Washington state, spread to Idaho and Montana and then north to Canada. It killed 87 people in the United States (mostly firefighters), made a hero of Ed Pulaski (inventor of the Pulaski fire tool, a combination pick and axe head on a long wooden handle)[36] and led to expansion and support for the United States Forest Service and, eventually, the warden service in Canada.

One of the more colourful men that Howard would have kept an eye on was Ike Brooks, who worked for the Brewsters in 1913. Bill Brewster met him while travelling in the United States. He was a rough bronc buster, who Bill felt would fit right in at the ranch, where breaking horses was a major part of the job. But it was about all he could do. His background at the time was working for the 101 Ranch, Wild West Show in Reno, Nevada, as a trick rider, as well as a bronc buster. There is a well-known picture in the Sundre Hotel, showing Ike riding a bronc with one foot in the stirrup and the other on the horse's flank. He must have had steel between his eyes and the body of Evel Knievel, as he was one of the wildest riders his old friend Bill Winter ever knew. He would "gallop over the steep hills, chasing horses, whipping his saddle horse all the way."[37] It is interesting to reflect on what Howard Sibbald thought of him, for he was "hard on horses" and broke them fast and rough. The horses inevitably came out wild and uncontrollable, very difficult to handle and mostly scared of riders. He would definitely not fit in with the type of horse breaking done on the ranch today. He managed to last quite a while, however, despite suffering severely from an injury he received to his back when a horse reared up and fell over on him. It must have bothered him, but apparently it did not slow him down.

Though Ike's boundless energy did not enhance his legacy as a horse breaker, it became legendary when he made an incredible ride to save a young girl's life. On December 4, 1915, Ike's stepdaughter developed appendicitis while staying at the ranch, now cut off by winter snows from any immediate medical help. There were no roads and the trails were snowbound and unbroken. Unable to move her to help, Ike rode for a doctor. He first rode to Sundre (83 km from the ranch), where he phoned a doctor in Olds. The doctor refused to make the trip, forcing Ike to ride back to the ranch, remount and head for Banff. After a perilous trip, he convinced Dr. Atkin to make the return trip with him, which was an epic of survival for both. The trail forced them to cross and recross several frozen mountain streams and rivers (21 in all) before reaching the ranch. On one near-fatal crossing, the doctor's horse plunged through the ice, nearly drowning him. A fire, a bite of cheese and a draught of whisky revived the determined doctor and they finally arrived to find the girl in critical condition.

There was no time to rest as the doctor turned the kitchen into an operating room. Before he set out on this madcap ride, he had made arrangements for his nurse to make her way via train and buggy to the ranch as quickly as possible. She arrived in time to help the doctor tend to the recovering patient, who had survived the operation. Both stayed on until she achieved full recovery. Though the exact distance and time are not recounted in the original story, one can assume the time was short (less than a week) and the distance was unfathomable for the conditions (166 km to Sundre, Olds and back, 205 km to Banff and back).[38]

Howard Sibbald's dedication to establishing the warden service may have been a factor in returning the Ya Ha Tinda to the national park. He had trained the men, established trails and built cabins for their extended stay in the mountains. This meant the park game guardians had greater presence in the field and often extended their patrols into the forest reserves bordering the park. One thing that galled Sibbald was the limitation on where he could build cabins. He considered establishing a cabin at the mouth of the Panther River, but, in his heart, he really wanted one built at the Ya Ha Tinda, now outside his jurisdiction. He argued, "The Ya Ha Tinda ranch (now Brewsters) is situated in the heart of the present game preserve, where the warden's headquarters should be. At present we have our headquarters at the mouth of the Panther River, which was as near in as we could winter horses successfully, as you will notice from the enclosed map."[39] It is not difficult to grasp, by reading between the lines, that there was no love lost between Sibbald and the Brewsters, and he positively coveted their ranch location. There is little doubt that Sibbald wanted the Ya Ha Tinda reinstated inside the

park, with the bonus of possibly removing the Brewsters altogether. He had a threefold argument: the Ya Ha Tinda was located in prime wildlife habitat; it was ideally situated for a warden operation centre for the eastern boundary of the park; and it had all the requirements for a horse ranch, which the wardens would need as their duties expanded. Unfortunately, it was the presence of horses on the ranch that people later saw as incompatible with wildlife protection.

To the Brewsters' (and Campbell's) dismay, with the help of J.B. Harkin's greater political pull, the national parks faction won out over the Forest Branch. It did not help the Brewsters' cause when their cowboys were caught poaching, but it was for another reason that the Brewsters felt they had lost the fight to keep their lease. When they first applied for the lease in 1904, the park superintendent, Howard Douglas, turned them down, giving the reason that horse grazing was incompatible with the park conservation interests. The following year, he did give them the lease, but it is not clear if he really agreed with the idea. There is some indication that he received direction to comply from Ottawa. The Brewsters were well-known Liberal supporters, who must have known former Albertan, Frank Oliver, and the minister of

Howard Sibbald
shaving on the trail.

the interior. The minister at one point even said he had instructed his staff to grant the lease.[40] Interestingly, it was never formally signed because the park (including the Ya Ha Tinda) had not yet been surveyed. With an unsigned but approved lease, the Brewsters were in a quasi-limbo state between being squatters and tenants.

The Brewsters were not known for being particularly subtle either. Their unwillingness to curb the poaching activities of their own men gave the impression they considered the ranch and its approach to be their domain and how they used it was their own concern.

In 1914, the boundaries of Rocky Mountains Park were again extended to include the Ya Ha Tinda, but the wheels of change turn slowly when the ultimate ruling body is on the other side of the country. By 1915, the new park superintendent, S.J. Clark, wrote specifically to Harkin, pointing out that the Brewsters were still running their ranch at the Ya Ha Tinda and were aggravating the situation by continuing to violate both provincial and federal game regulations. He requested that their lease be terminated immediately. Harkin again took up the grail and a memorandum was sent to Campbell, requesting that the lease be cancelled. At this point there was some doubt about the validity of said lease in the first place. But by this time there was no lease to be found, and the Brewsters were given a notice to vacate the land and its premises. The reason parks wanted them gone was because of the poaching concerns, but Pat Brewster later gave another reason for their expulsion.

> *My brother Jim was sitting in the Palliser Hotel one day when R.B. Bennett (future Prime Minister of Canada) came by and put out his hand to shake Jim's. Jim said, "Go on, you pot-bellied old bugger." Bennett remembered the insult. About two years later, a horse wrangler for one of Jim's camping parties killed a deer out of season for meat for the camp, something of a common procedure in those days. A park warden happened along and placed the wrangler under arrest. Bennett got word of the case and followed it to the court. When the judgment came down, it was that the Brewsters would lose all rights to their lease and remove their stock from the Ya Ha Tinda.[41]*

Bennett, who was a partner of the Bennett Jones law firm, was known for his quick temper and harbouring a grudge. It is not mentioned what influence Bennett had on the outcome, but he did attend the trial almost daily.

Men in front of log cabin at the Ya Ha Tinda Brewster Ranch, Alberta.

Wrangler breaking
horses at the
Brewster Ranch.

In the end, the Brewsters lost the case, which resulted in their losing the ranch. Possibly, Douglas had a change of heart about grazing horses in the park and became more concerned with poaching activities. Either way, the Brewsters barely got their animals moved before Sibbald was setting up headquarters and turning the place into a horse ranch for the warden service.

CHAPTER 2
THE GOLDEN YEARS

I'd just stand and look at this beautiful country – just like a huge bowl and five
passes to get out up and down the Red, up the Panther, over the Clearwater
and down the James River.... I don't think you can get a more delightful way
of spending your time if you like the peaceful way of mountain life.
—Nellie Murphy, "A History with National Park Wardens, 1919–1950"

The Brewsters had the run of the Ya Ha Tinda for 11 years and were reluctant to leave. To this day, they still maintain they at least had squatter's rights to the place.[42] Though told to leave in 1915, they made no effort to do so. The problem was finally turned over to the federal Department of Justice in 1916 to get them moving.[43] Perhaps the family thought the decision to evict them might be reversed in their favour if they dragged it out long enough. With the constant wrangling over who had final authority over the land, this might have worked. However, by 1917, the boundaries were finalized and they had no choice but to vacate that year. By that summer, warden Howard (Fat) Cain had already moved into the buildings the Brewsters had built, with instructions to "hold down" the ranch for the government. There must have been some residual unease about whether the Brewsters would actually leave despite the eviction notice.

The biggest task for the Brewsters was to find and catch all the horses and cattle that had roamed freely on those vast meadows and timbered draws. The horses were particularly problematic; after years of rough breaking by men like Ike Brooks, most of them were understandably afraid of people. There were many young unbroken horses that had not been as much as halter-broken, let alone exposed to any sort of handling by people. They had also been allowed to run free most of the year when

Bill Logan and Colonel Scott in front of a tipi on the way to the Ya Ha Tinda.

not being used in the summer and knew the land much better than the men brought in to round them up. Though there would always be wild horses in the area, it was important to remove the Brewster horses before the Ya Ha Tinda could be developed as a horse ranch for the warden service.

The story of rounding up these animals is quite colourful. It was well known by every wrangler, guide and outfitter that the Brewsters had to get off the Ya Ha Tinda that summer, and one man felt there could be a profit in it. Canada had already endured huge losses in the Great War that had started in the summer of 1914 and, by 1917, the war department was in dire need of horses. The war effort had already exhausted all surplus horses and the farmers and ranchers had none to spare. No one knew how long the war would last, leaving the government little choice but to pay top dollar for what horses they could find.

The problem was resolved when Norman Luxton, along with P.D. Bowlen (owner of the Bar C Ranch) and Bill Logan (a local rancher on the Red Deer River), decided to buy the horses from the Brewsters for $1,000.00. They felt it well worth their time to buy the horses, round them up and drive them to Cochrane, where the government was paying up to $95 a head per horse (in 1909, the Brewsters were running

150 horses on the ranch). "Whispering" Dave McDougall bought the cattle with the same idea. The profit (unknown) may not have been as substantial, but 100 head of cattle would be easier to find and drive to market than the semi-wild horses. Meanwhile, Luxton saw it as an adventure as much as a profitable scheme and felt if he even brought back 50 horses, it would be worth his while.

Luxton was an adventurous man who earned the nickname "Mr. Banff" by investing in the town. He had a background in newspapers and when he finally settled down in Banff, he published the *Crag and Canyon* newspaper, ran a curio store and eventually founded the King Edward Hotel and the Luxton Museum. He did not have a substantial background in chasing or catching wild horses, however, and knew he needed men with experience. One wonders if this was foremost in his mind when he met Fred Scott at the Palliser Hotel in Calgary, who was lunching there with a friend of his. He soon found out that Scott was convalescing from the war but had picked up two years of experience with horses at the Jarboe Horse and Cattle Ranch near Blindloss, a small prairie town in southern Alberta. He immediately invited Scott to join the expedition to the Ya Ha Tinda, thinking, "It'll settle your nerves and make a new man of you."

He lightly added, "All you need is your bedroll and riding clothes." Considering where they were going for the next few months, Luxton was either master of the understatement or had no idea how remote the Ya Ha Tinda was and how challenging the work would be in that rough country.[44]

The next man Luxton hired was Jack Fuller, a 17-year-old young man who was raised on a horse ranch near Innisfail, Alberta. Jack had been working for a big steam company near Acme, close to the Saskatchewan border, when he decided it was not for him. With the thought, "What the hell am I doing here?" he picked up his pay, mounted his "little Pinto Crown horse" and rode back to Morley (via the Bar C Ranch).[45] There he ran into Luxton, who was heading to Banff to make arrangements for the roundup. When Luxton offered him the job to come along as wrangler, he jumped at the chance. Despite his young age, he had a lot of experience with horses and immediately advised Luxton to bring along halters, hobbles and bells. Fuller had a somewhat gentler approach to breaking horses than the Brewster cowboys.

When Fuller met Scott in Banff, Luxton explained that the young soldier "was going along just for the ride."[46] The convalescing part was probably not brought up. Fuller was

familiar with Ya Ha Tinda country and had some reservations about the experience his boss and new companion had for the arduous trip ahead. To his relief, an old friend with considerable experience at chasing horses in rough country showed up just before the train left for Morley. George Harrison was a guide and an outfitter who had been hired by Dave McDougall to help with the cattle-drive part of the expedition. They would all be travelling together to the Ya Ha Tinda, which pleased Fuller as Harrison was a good man on the trail.

Luxton felt he was well prepared with his buckskin jacket and moose hide pants the Stoneys had made for him, but he had not counted on the federal government agent relieving him of his half-dozen bottles of whiskey stashed for the trip. The man could smell whiskey a mile away, particularly around the Indian reserve, where it was illegal. Luxton had to call in a few favours but managed to avoid a court appointment for the offence, though it meant leaving without the whiskey.

They finally got away with tack, tents, personal gear and enough food for a month. Scott must have taken advice from Fuller or Harrison to bring warm clothes, a slicker and a good hat, as the snow was still on the ground when they left Morley. They had ten heavily laden pack horses, giving Scott numerous occasions to perfect tying the diamond hitch. He writes, "Here I had my first lesson in throwing and tying the diamond hitch an indispensable education in the use of pack horses for the mountain trails. Inexperienced pack horses may wander off the narrow trail and get tangled against brush or trees until retrieved, so packing had to be well done."[47] The 80-mile ride through virgin pine forests often tight, dark and narrow, was as new to him as it was for most of the horses.

Jack Fuller's account of the first day does not mention the Aboriginal men who accompanied them to the Bar C Ranch, but they made an impression on Scott as exceptionally good riders. Here they replenished supplies and horses then pushed on to Bill Logan's ranch on "The Big Red" – a local name for the Red Deer River. It is aptly named, as this river can be notoriously high and wild with the spring runoff. From there, it was a 20-mile ride to the Ya Ha Tinda.

When the party got to the ranch, they were surprised to find two other local ranchers there who knew the country well. Boney Thompson and Archie Howard had just returned from the Clearwater River, where they had been hunting for elk.[48] Park warden, Howard Cain, and his family were also there and living in the Brewster cabin. For a country usually devoid of people, it must have felt like a country fair to Howard Cain's wife, Clara. Clara was the first woman to reside at the Ya Ha Tinda, and she found it very isolated with only her husband and son (the men soon nicknamed him "Timberline") for company. The visits by the men who passed through were few and far between and the women even fewer. Her "home on the range" was the small dingy log cabin left by the Brewster cowboys that she had fixed up with the few resources available to her. Nonetheless, she was an excellent cook and never failed to cheerfully deliver hearty meals. Clara was known for her hospitality. She enjoyed the company of anyone who visited, particularly if they agreed to play five hundred, her favourite card game. She never failed to win, no matter how hard her opponents tried to cheat.

During that particular horse drive, Clara also picked up the colourful nickname of "Cayuse Clara." She was an excellent horsewoman, which was probably what attracted her to life on the Ya Ha Tinda, and rode extensively when given the chance. Luxton had promised her "the pick of the bunch" from any of the horses brought in, and she never failed to show up to look them over. She wanted a saddle horse of her own and not one supplied by the government. She earned the nickname after being kicked in the head by a horse she had come down to inspect in a squeeze chute. The narrow log enclosure allowed them to work on the horses with minimal harm to themselves or the animal. Clara had hurried down, hoping to get a good look at him. As she leaned over to peer at the horse between the logs, the wild little horse's foot suddenly shot out from under the corral fence and "stood Clara on her head,"

hence the name "Cayuse." In the end, Clara did get her horse, a nice four-year-old filly that gave her little trouble.[49]

Once the Luxton party arrived at the ranch, they were happy to accept the generous offer to use Howard Cain's cabin for accommodation. There was also a barn and a couple of small corrals. Jack Fuller convinced Luxton to hire Boney Thompson for the roundup, as his knowledge of the country and horsemanship made him invaluable. By now, Fuller realized that Luxton had no idea how hard it would be to corral the Brewster horses, and the extra man and horse were needed. The first part of the month was spent in building corrals and wing fences to help haze and hold the horses they would bring in. Once that was accomplished, the hard part of catching the cagy animals began. Finding them was not hard, but getting close enough to run them in the right direction was a real challenge. A man on foot did not disturb them too much, but one on horseback had them vacating the country before they were barely spotted. Though Fuller must have wondered how much help Scott would be with his limited horse-chasing experience, he soon came to appreciate what a great addition he proved to be.

We all got a big bang out of Scott "the flying man" as we called him. He was good help with everything and although he never took part in any of our gallops, he always went along, taking pictures and always seemed to pop up in the right place at the right time. Several times, a bunch would be making a break or a getaway. We would be racing over rocks and fallen timber, trying to head the horses off and Scott would pop up in front of them with his camera and they would turn.[50]

After several days of building fences and corrals, they were ready for the first drive. They caught 30 head the first day with ease, but every horse caught from then on was hard and dangerous work. Though Fuller does not recall Scott being involved in any of the big drives, he did get caught up on one chase he never forgot. Because of his inexperience, Scott was usually sent to some strategic point where he could jump out and haze the herd back toward the corrals if it looked like they were making a break for the bush. He was in the process of doing just that, riding a small saddle horse named Lally, when he got swept up in the chase on the final run to the corrals. He recalls, "From there I started on one of the most amazing rides I ever made, shouting aloud as I dashed down through and over fallen timber."[51]

Packing building materials from the Ya Ha Tinda.

The men were always flushing the horses out of deep timber where the ground was perilous, covered in fallen timber and boulders and laced with sudden deep draws, carved by small creeks. It took a seasoned, keen-eyed, swift horse to take the punishment of these drives. Not all survived. Jack Fuller lost a good mount he deeply cared for when it broke a leg running down a steep embankment.

Scott also saw the evidence of the brutality in horse roundups of the past. It is unlikely that very many people used Ike Brook's method of trailing horses out of that timbered country. Ike thought the best way to keep horses together was to tie them in pairs by head and tail. This was totally disastrous for the semi-wild horses that spooked and ran off, tied together. Most died as they became hopelessly tangled in the deadfall. White bones, with remnants of old rope, were the last evidence of this misbegotten idea. Jack Fuller did not have much use for Ike as a ranch hand, though he did admit he seemed to be able to ride anything. He comments, "What Ike didn't know about ranching would fill volumes … nor did he know much about breaking horses. He whip-broke everything!"[52]

Scott seems slightly diffident when he sums up his experience: "I realize that some parts of our expedition may not make a pleasant story.

I was a guest with no authority and I am not defending the methods which were used, nor am I being unduly critical, but I have merely provided a factual description of a roundup as it actually occurred."[53] In the end, Luxton and Bowlen made their money back after beefing up the horses with feed before selling them to the government. Clara's experience living at the Ya Ha Tinda did not last long. Howard Cain quit the ranch that year and was replaced by three other men, now officially called park wardens. This new identification was the outcome of the past confusion over the role of forest rangers and park game guardians. When the park recovered much of the land it lost in 1911, Harkin felt it was time to solidify the authority of those enforcing the regulations. He maintained, "Forest rangers are not suitable for the duties of game guardians" because their functions were incompatible with the intent of preservation in the national park. He declared that the fire and game wardens were to be appointed as "wardens." No official reason was given for using this name other than speculation he wished to have this new service be distinct from provincial rangers and their American cousins, known as park rangers. Whatever the reason, the warden service was now fully recognized and would go on to function in many capacities over the next 100 years.

In 1917, however, it was a fledgling force, with a focused intent on establishing the trails and cabins needed to enforce the game regulations of the expanding federal parks in the West. Howard Sibbald had been tasked with establishing the warden service, and, though his hub of operation remained in Banff, for what was still then called Rocky Mountains National Park, he had five other parks and reserves to staff and develop as well. (There were the Yoho and Glacier national park reserves in 1886, Waterton Lakes National Park in 1895 and Jasper National Park in 1907). During this period, he often hired legendary individuals in their own right to run these parks. Men like Kootenai Brown in Waterton, Bill Peyto in Banff and Lewis Swift in Jasper. All of these parks would require horses, and supplying these mounts would eventually become the purpose of the vast pastures of the Ya Ha Tinda.[54]

45

Once the transfer of the Ya Ha Tinda from the Brewsters to Rocky Mountains National Park was accomplished, the work of establishing the ranch as a wintering and training ground for park horses began. Achieving this goal happened slowly, starting first with making the Ya Ha Tinda the headquarters of the northeast quadrant of the park. All of the parks ran on a district system employed to help manage the vast areas the wardens had to patrol. The Ya Ha Tinda was well located to be the headquarters for this distant corner of the park, from which the wardens travelled easily to patrol cabins established in previous years.

When the Ya Ha Tinda was finally under the jurisdiction of Rocky Mountains National Park, there were only five wardens working for Sibbald. He asked for and got 12 more the following year. The number of horses initially wintering at the ranch was small, with only 17 wardens on staff in the park. With few horses to look after, the first order of business was to upgrade the facilities on the ranch. Wardens Jack Bevan, Scotty Wright and Jack Warren, stationed at the ranch at this time, concentrated on relocating the ranch headquarters to higher ground north of the Red Deer River, on the east bank of Scalp Creek. By 1920, they had a substantial four-room cabin, a barn, a small implement shed and the corrals. Jack

Bevan stayed on as district warden until 1923, when Art Allison replaced him. Allison seems to have run the place on his own until Percy Woodworth joined him in 1927. In 1929, Cliff Murphy joined the staff at the ranch, where he would stay with his wife Nellie until 1947.[55]

Historian Jim Taylor referred to these early years as the "Golden Years" because the ranch was considered to be under the protective umbrella of the federal government and operated "in a fairly uniform way as a game preserve, warden operations and horse ranch."[56] The resident warden was responsible for not only the ranch but also the backcountry of the northeast districts of the park, which required regular patrols. Though the work was considerable, the winter months would have been long and tedious. The wardens were stationed in the backcountry year-round on their own, with rare trips out to see friends and family. The records from that period are basically nonexistent, and little is known about the private lives of these men. In lifestyle, they could be considered much like the lone mountain men of the early West. They would have been competent, self-sufficient individuals who could adapt well to the isolation.

The ranch really took shape under the direction of warden Cliff Murphy when he took charge in 1929. Murphy may have loved the

Superintendent P.J. Jennings at Dormer Cabin on the Panther River.

place as soon as he got there, or maybe it grew on him the longer he stayed. It certainly melded with his personality, for he was a quiet, shy man. Either way, he would remain for the next 19 years. Though the operation of the ranch remained unaltered, a very significant change did occur politically and geographically the year following his arrival. In 1930, the federal Transfer of Resources Act irrevocably changed the future and security of the Ya Ha Tinda as a government horse ranch. The earlier reduction of parks lands in 1911 proved the federal government in Ottawa had difficulty digesting the

complexity of preserving the flora and fauna of the natural environment and the (apparently empty) land that was required for this. The Alberta government merely saw vast tracts of uninhabited land that were full of natural resources, if only it could claim them. This was partially the result of the eternal conundrum of justifying the expense of the park against the revenue it brought in. "Use without abuse" was Harkin's constant nightmare and one that would never truly be resolved.[57] National parks belonged to the people who had the right to enjoy them, but that alone destroyed the wilderness so vital to the survival of the flora and fauna the parks sought to protect. Not only was there a philosophy of exploitation of natural resources entrenched among the bureaucrats but there was also an appeasement attitude toward newly created provinces, particularly in the West. Perhaps the federal government felt if it did not share the wealth, there would be a western coalition urging separation from the Dominion. All through the 1920s, the Department of the Interior negotiated with the Alberta government to transfer many of these natural resources to the province. The squabbling over the resources on the Ya Ha Tinda, from many interests, would be endemic from then on.

When the Transfer of Resources Act became legislated, J.B. Harkin was still the commissioner of the Dominion Parks Branch, which administered all of the national parks in Canada. Harkin's own philosophy was one of preservation and protection of the parks, but he was faced with a difficult choice when the act came into being. Up to this point, the removal of resources from the parks had been more than tolerated, if not completely overlooked. Mining, logging and even hydroelectric development was permitted. Harkin disagreed with this use of the parks as a source of resource extraction, but he was given little

backing by the federal government. Under the new act, Harkin could eliminate all resource exploitation in the park if he agreed to fix new park boundaries that would eliminate a considerable portion of the eastern part of the park. In return, the remainder of the park would receive full protection of the federal government. Thinking this was for the greater good, Harkin agreed to reduce the boundaries of Rocky Mountains National Park. R.W. Cautley, the Dominion land surveyor, had the difficult job of determining where the park boundary adjustments would be made. Cautley was instructed to focus on the eastern slopes of the Rockies for these cuts, as the province knew that was where the valuable timber, mineral wealth and water resources were. One could see coal seams blackening the strata in the hills of the Ya Ha Tinda, a resource the province was always looking for. He was also told to eliminate areas that did not come up to the standard of beauty found in the rest of the national park.

Cautley eliminated all of the land east of, and including, Canmore, largely due to coal-bearing rock formations, and then turned his scrutinizing attention to the Red Deer and Clearwater river watersheds. He eliminated much of this valley, including the Ya Ha Tinda, on the basis that it did not meet the scenic requirements of a national park. Maybe he did not actually get to the Ya Ha Tinda, undeniably one of the most beautiful jewels in the original park. By the time Cautley was finished, the ranch was back to an indeterminate status. Cautley even argued the Ya Ha Tinda was not worth keeping as a grazing area, as it did not appear to be cost-effective.[58]

This move caught everyone off balance. The ever-watchful Brewsters, upon hearing the ranch was now part of the province, petitioned for their old title to be reinstated. Taylor writes, "Having heard that the ranch was about to be ceded from the park, James Brewster wrote the department asking if he could obtain title to the land." The park was alarmed when it realized it could lose the ranch, as Ottawa seemed happy to get rid of it. R.S. Stronach, the park superintendent (likely egged on by Sibbald), asked Ottawa to preserve it as grazing land. Someone must have listened, as an order-in-council declared that the Ya Ha Tinda ranch would be set aside "for the use of the Dominion Parks Branch for grazing purposes."[59] It essentially became a federal reserve within a provincial forest reserve.

The whole issue of giving land back to the province must have triggered a thoughtful review of why the parks were there in the first place. Harkin would have had a voice in

establishing the National Parks Act, which revised the boundaries and gave the park a new set of rules and a new name: Banff National Park.

Though this was a very significant development for the Ya Ha Tinda, it did not seem to affect the day-to-day operations at the ranch. The biggest change to the functional life of the wardens on the ground was the land they were now responsible for. Interestingly, the redrawing of the lines provided very little direction with regard to the game regulations. That little conundrum, though, would not be challenged until much later.

Cliff Murphy was not the sort of man to enter the fray of politics, and his isolation on the ranch gave him little opportunity to follow the machinations of officials at the ministerial level in Ottawa. All that really mattered to him was the work at hand and what his responsibilities were. He was happy on this land in the small house built in 1920. When the momentous transfer act came into being, Murphy had only been working at the ranch for over a year. But he loved it there and had no reason to think he would be asked to leave any time soon. In this, he was correct.

Though Murphy spent most of his time on the ranch, it was clearly necessary to travel out to Banff from time to time, if not for his

rare need for company, then at least for supplies and a break from work. Though he was shy, he became attracted to a young lady working for Gus Baracos at the Banff Café. The lady was Nellie (Babe) Riviere. Nellie was born and raised in Pincher Creek, where she learned ranching skills from her parents, Nellie Gladstone and Henri Riviere. When she met Murphy, she was living with her uncle, Wallace Gladstone, a park warden in Banff National Park. She was already quite familiar with the duties of a town park warden but not those of a district warden. Nevertheless, she was attracted to the shy Murphy, especially when he decided to court her. Little did she know what life would be like for her when they married in 1933, since that would mean moving to the Ya Ha Tinda. The last woman to make a dent in the place was "Cayuse" Clara, 16 years earlier.

Fortunately for Nellie, she had the skills and the fortitude to survive the impact that bordered on culture shock when seeing the small home cabin for the first time. Though Murphy was living in the log house that had been built in 1920, his bachelor housekeeping had not made the place particularly homey. Nellie's first reaction was to sit down and cry. After the long trip in, the revelation of how isolated the place really was settled on her like a weight. Nellie was 27 when she saw the Ya Ha Tinda

for the first time, but by then she was already extremely proficient as a cook and homemaker. She was skilled with hand tools, rifles and ranch stock and had ridden most of her life. Her reaction was to dig in and turn the place into a real home. With soap, water, paint and curtains, she turned the place into a welcome home.

Other things that helped make life a bit easier for her included getting in a well with a hand pump. Though it meant hauling water to the house, it was better than bringing it up from the creek. Murphy took his husbandly duties seriously, if quietly, and he soon built a windmill to power an electric generator that provided electric lights. Somehow he managed to trail in two cows for fresh milk. They even had a battery-powered radio that they used sparingly. Though the privy was still outside, there was a tub that could be filled with hot water from the large kettles singing on the wood stove. The house still remained drafty and hard to heat in the winter, but Nellie did not mind that. The beauty of the ranch and even the spring snow squalls delighted her. She was one of the first people to write about daily life on the Ya Ha Tinda, and in one passage she gives homage to the changing weather: "We had blustery weather and I loved these snow squalls. They'd last about 15 minutes and I'd grab my coat and hat and go out for a walk, the snow blowing in my face, the ground all white and in 20 minutes it would all be good again." She loved living in the solitude of the mountains: "I did a lot of walking. I'd just stand and look at this beautiful country – just like a huge bowl and five passes to get out – up or down the Red; up the Panther, over the Clearwater; and down the James River. I don't think you can get a more delightful way of spending time if you like the peaceful way of mountain life. I climbed up every hill and down every coulee."[60]

Though Nellie loved the ranch, in the 1930s it was still very remote, and much of her writing reflects the intense loneliness it could bring. These long periods would be punctuated by weeks of hectic spring and fall activity, particularly later, when the horse herd began to grow. But during those first years, Nellie kept the boredom at bay by accompanying her husband on his patrols and helping with all the work required on the ranch. She had only been there two months when she faced her first big challenge of helping with the annual spring horse drive to Banff. Every spring, the Banff horses had to be rounded up and trailed back to the Banff range for the summer's work. This would be a routine that would last until roads were finally built to the ranch in the mid-1940s and they could be trucked out. In the fall, the reverse would happen and the Banff wardens would get together to trail all the horses back to the Ya Ha Tinda for the winter.

The Ya Ha Tinda was a little less remote than when the Brewsters ran the place because, by the 1930s, a phone line finally reached the ranch. This link to the outside world began in 1914 as Banff's line cabins were established and was almost complete by 1933. It was a forestry phone system that ran throughout all the parks and its maintenance was a major part of the backcountry warden's job. The trail to the Ya Ha Tinda was also becoming very well established due to two major fires that swept the country in 1920 and again in 1929. The trail up the Cascade and over Snow Creek Summit to the Red Deer River, and thence to the Ya Ha Tinda, would eventually become a road built primarily for forest fire suppression.[61]

Her first horse trip to Banff probably surprised Nellie with how difficult and dangerous trailing the horses back in the spring could be. In 1933, western Canada still experienced severe winters, and the spring snow stayed long and deep in the passes. Murphy made arrangements for two wardens to come in to help with the drive, but that meant the men first had to ride to the ranch. Ulysses LaCasse and Jack Naylor made it to Cuthead Cabin, but the snow was so deep that Naylor hurt his back and had to return to Banff. LaCasse carried on to Windy

Cabin and phoned to say it was too deep to make it over Snow Creek Summit and would be coming to the ranch by way of the Panther River. Murphy and Nellie waited up for LaCasse to arrive at the ranch. He finally showed up at 12:30 that night, worn out. Nellie went with the men to take the horses back to Banff the next day on a trip she would never forget.

Next morning they rounded up all the horses and put them in the holding pasture. Then portions of the herd were brought into the corral where Cliff separated those that were to be taken to Banff. Finally the horses were all sorted out and the men were tired. We had a big supper and went to bed early. We had a tough ride ahead of us. I had the pack boxes all packed and ready. Ulysses told us the Panther was open in the middle and that was no good. There must be ten or more crossings this dangerous when the creek is high. There had been ten packhorses lost in this creek and they landed on the banks where the Panther flows into the Red Deer three miles from the ranger station.

We had a big breakfast and all the horses were in the corral. We packed the packhorses, got on the horses we were riding, let the packhorses loose and Cliff opened the gate and hollered, "Come on boys!" and they all followed. Ulysses and I rode at the end of the herd and it sure didn't take long to get to the Corners Cabin. There we started this crossing back and forth of the creek all the way to Windy. We had to jump off the ice into the creek and jump out, not much fun.

We made good time and reached Windy Cabin at two thirty that afternoon. All the horses were in the two corrals. We had lunch and the men went around too check the fence then turned the horses loose in the pasture. We had a big supper and went to bed. Tomorrow would be a hard day.

We didn't hurry thinking we'd give the sun a chance to soften the snow up a bit. We ate breakfast, the men got the horses in, I packed the packhorses and was ready. We started with Cliff leading, Ulysses and I following the herd. We didn't go far when we got into deep snow three to four feet of it, Cliff wiggling close to the trees where it was not so deep. We were somewhere near the trail but up on higher ground. The horses were making a trench then finally noticed we were going down-slope toward Snow Creek then we came to the hill, which was very steep. We could see Cliff way below with the horses following all strung out nicely. The hill was slippery as grease where the horses had gone down. Ulysses said, "I'm going to walk." I said, "Not me! I'll just slide down on the horse as I'd be on my butt if I tried to walk." Ulysses said, "Okay, I'll follow you." We were lucky our horses didn't fall.

We were soon at Cuthead Cabin, changed horses and were off to Stoney Creek Cabin, then on to Bankhead, which we reached at two-thirty that afternoon. From there I'd get a ride with Bill Potts for the remaining five miles into Banff.[62]

The summer would have passed quickly for Nellie, with her homemaking and helping Murphy with his patrols, and managing the ranch and entertaining (feeding large meals to) the crews that came in to help with summer haying. There were also regular visits from the various patrolling wardens stationed in the park proper. Throughout this period, the ranch remained central to the warden patrol network and was administered through the Banff Park Office. Cliff Murphy was still a full-time warden and continued to assume the duties of a warden, though the majority of his responsibilities were taken up with managing the ranch. Throughout his tenure, he continued to patrol and clear deadfall off the trails and keep up the maintenance of the phone line.

Spring was the busiest time of the year at the Ya Ha Tinda, once the horses were rounded up.

The horses had to be shod, branded and their abilities assessed before trailing them back to Banff for the summer. It was always a big event each spring at the Banff warden headquarters when the horses came back from the ranch for the summer and fall seasons. Here they were sorted out for district or town work. The wardens from the other 12 districts in Banff relished the first opportunity to visit their colleagues after communicating only by phone all winter. They spent almost the whole year in the backcountry districts and the spring rendezvous in Banff to gather their horses was a significant reprieve from that solitary job.[63]

Howard Sibbald had done an excellent job in establishing and expanding the warden service over the 15 years he worked for the federal government. He had gone on to become superintendent of Kootenay National Park and retired in 1932. By then, the national parks in the West had wardens patrolling and maintaining trails, cabins and a phone line that connected them to park headquarters by a precarious line of wires strung between trees and makeshift poles.

With everyone out from the bush, the wardens were required to attend Cuthead College. This was the annual training that all wardens got in firefighting, mountain rescue, wildlife management and law enforcement. During this time, Nellie took it easy, visiting friends and picking up supplies for the coming summer.

Under the tender care of Cliff Murphy, the Ya Ha Tinda evolved into the horse ranch Sibbald and Douglas had envisioned. It became the heart of the warden service's operations, as horses were essential to almost all aspects of the job, with the protection of the boundaries and wildlife being the first priority. When Murphy first came to the ranch, only 60 head of horses from Banff wintered there. The remaining 40 head used by the park wintered in Banff on the range near the old horse barns. The other parks made different arrangements – Yoho horses wintered around Cochrane, while Jasper and Waterton kept their horses on pastures within the park. By the 1940s, however, it was decided to winter the Kootenay, Yoho and Glacier horses at the Ya Ha Tinda as well. This increased the size of the herd wintering on the ranch considerably. They wintered up to 125–150 horses, a number that varied little for several years.

The park horses actually shared the superb range conditions in and around the Ya Ha Tinda with outfitter horses. Nellie Murphy recorded in 1930 that outfitters such as Ray Legace, Jack Thomas and Jimmy Simpson kept horses in the area as well. These were outfitters who had horse concessions in the park. Not only did the

wardens have a spring roundup but the other outfitters would be there as well, rounding up their horses for the summer. Some of them kept horses further down the Red Deer, but Legace always kept his horses to the south of the ranch and camped each spring close to the southeast boundary. The sound of cowboys whooping and yelling as they brought the stampeding horses back to camp could be heard bouncing off the hills during the few open weeks of spring before the Red Deer got too high to cross safely. Each spring these horses would be trailed back to Lake Louise via the Red Deer and Pipestone rivers.

Though this added to the number of horses wintering on or around the Ya Ha Tinda ranch and its surrounding open grasslands, there is no mention of concern over forage. Nellie recorded seeing a lot of mule deer and bighorn sheep up until 1936, when an actinomycosis epidemic decimated the sheep. In the later 1930s, she said, "We hardly saw sheep anymore on the big hillside."[64] They frequently saw black bears, grizzlies and cougars. Even wolves were seen from time to time. But it was not until 1942 that elk were recorded on the ranch. A small herd of 50 bull elk was mentioned in the wildlife counts for the first time. Even the sheep recovered quickly, as noted the same year when 100 sheep were again seen on the hillside.

An early effort was made in 1937–1938 to reintroduce bison to the ranch. Murphy met Jack Rae, the horse farrier/trucker for Banff at the time, and loaded two, two-year-old yearlings onto a horse-drawn wagon. One can only imagine the difficulty of that trip back to the ranch under the road conditions of the day. It was not a successful venture. Once the buffalo matured, their nomadic nature kicked in and off they went. They proceeded up the Red Deer River as far as the Cyclone District warden cabin. When they then ventured east, as far as Sundre, the ranchers had enough and they were eventually caught and penned up at Nordegg, northwest of Sundre. Their ultimate fate was probably a good meal on a rancher's plate.

Though the winters were long and lonely for Nellie, she did get the odd chance to show her skills as a cook and get in some visiting over card games. Most of the visitors in the winter were trappers. This was a godsend for Nellie, as Murphy was a notoriously quiet man. She could carry on a conversation with herself for months without interruption. During the winter of 1942, they had more permanent company when Cougar Long and Dewey Browning spent part of the winter in the bunkhouse, trapping squirrels. They would meet each evening to play poker, with a squirrel skin being the measure of currency. "Squirrel hides, which were worth about 10 cents, were used as betting tender."[65]

Nellie also recalls that the Stoneys from Nordegg used to come through the ranch in the summer and camp at Bighorn Creek, below the waterfalls. They were returning from the Calgary Stampede and Banff Indian Days. It must have brought an insight into what their life had been like, before they lost their home hunting grounds at the Ya Ha Tinda at the turn of the century.

As the horse herd increased, haying became a bigger part of the job every summer. The Murphys seeded brome, crested wheat grass and oats. They usually got extra help from Banff, either a trail crew or seasonal wardens from town. Nellie noted that though they had all this tame grass, it was the wild bunch grass they cut that the horses thrived on.

During the Murphys' stay at the Ya Ha Tinda, there was no organized horse-breeding program, but with the horses running unfettered on the open meadows during the fall and winter, crossbreeding with local wild horses was not uncommon. Quite often a colt or two (or more) would come in with the spring roundup. Murphy called these "catch colts" and allowed them to stay with their dams. These he would break himself and, if they were good, they

would soon join the stable of Banff horses. There were a couple of occasions when stallions (Many Colours was used in 1947) were "borrowed" from outfitters like Jimmy Simpson or Tom Harvey for breeding a good mare. But this was quite informal. A breeding program was not entertained by the park at the time but would play a big role in the future.

Cliff Murphy had dedicated himself to the cultivation of the Ya Ha Tinda as a horse ranch for the warden service, but he never forgot that he was a warden himself. He continued to operate the ranch as though it were headquarters for the Red Deer River District, even though the ranch was not in the park. No one questioned this and so remained under the illusion the Ya Ha Tinda was under protection from hunting. Thus, because this was not challenged, the 18 years of Murphy's tenure at the ranch marked the longest and most stable period the ranch experienced. There was even stirring in Ottawa to reincorporate the ranch into the national park after Ian McTaggart-Cowan completed a wildlife study with that recommendation in 1943. Wildlife numbers had grown under the misperception that the Ya Ha Tinda was actually federally protected land. McTaggart-Cowan was appalled, however, by the predator control that was so widely enforced by the warden service. He stated that overcrowding was more of a hazard to the ungulate population than predation by wolves.[66] Typically, none of these ideas dented the mind of anyone of sufficient seniority to make any real change to the status of the Ya Ha Tinda.

It is interesting that Murphy himself would cause the focus to shift to the status of the ranch as a game sanctuary, when, in 1944, he charged two hunters for poaching. Taylor writes, "It seemed that no one within the parks organization was aware that the wardens had no jurisdiction to enforce the national parks regulations on the Ya Ha Tinda."[67] Provincial forests that fell under the provincial game regulations surrounded the ranch, but there was no fence to delineate the boundaries of the Ya Ha Tinda. With this clarification, the province took the view that the park had no authority to prohibit hunting on the ranch. Suddenly, everyone became interested in how the land should

be regulated. Bruce Mitchell, who was the chief park warden of Banff at the time, wanted to preserve the land for game protection but was not that keen on keeping it as a horse ranch. The superintendent wanted all forms of protection, including keeping it as a horse ranch. They lobbied Ottawa for support and finally got some attention. Once again, the federal government approached the province about a possible land exchange, hoping to open up some avenue of dialogue. The province unceremoniously squashed all dialogue when it refused to even acknowledge any communication on the subject with Ottawa.

Somehow, the ubiquitous Brewsters seemed to have a finger in the pie. Mitchell had approached Eric Huestis, the Alberta Fish and Game commissioner for the province, about declaring the Ya Ha Tinda a protected area for game. He was roundly criticized for having any idea that the federal government should meddle with land belonging to the province, with Huestis stating, "The Ya Ha Tinda Ranch area was Alberta Provincial Property." Huestis goes on to complain, "Banff National Park is too large now, and what does the Dominion Government want with more game preserves?" Astonishingly, he adds, "Why had Brewsters been paying the Provincial government lease rental on the ranch area all these years." This

J. Marie Nylund

must have been confusing to Mitchell, who seems to have had little liking for Huestis (and visa versa). When the Brewsters were evicted from the park in 1917, there had been no evidence of a lease agreement with anyone, and there was no record of payment for the time they did run livestock on the ranch. Huestis was certainly aware of the grudge between the Brewsters and the federal government over the appropriation of "their land" at that time and seemed to harbour some resentment of his own on that past decision. Any further movement

on this matter came to an abrupt halt when the provincial government refused to acknowledge any communication from Ottawa, claiming it had "lost the file."[68]

After Murphy lost the poaching case, the province administered the game regulations on the Ya Ha Tinda, but it still did not have the manpower to make its presence known. The wardens continued to patrol and monitor the ranch as though nothing had changed. There were no more reports of poaching, so they must have had some effect, though the stability of the past 18 years eroded after Murphy retired three years later in 1947.[69]

Though Mitchell was not a supporter of the Ya Ha Tinda as a horse ranch, he was an effective chief park warden. His son Randy Mitchell, later to work for parks himself, sums up his father's tenure from the copious journals he kept during all his years as a warden: "The journals suggest that Bruce Mitchell was a fair yet determined 'hands on' Chief Park Warden."[70] He worked long hours, with rarely a day off, and spent considerable time travelling park roads and trails, either by vehicle, horse or foot (skis and snowshoes in the winter). He did not spend much time in his office.

Horses turned out for the winter.

Horses running in
winter on the ranch.

PHOTO BY MARIE NYLUND.

J. Marie Nylund

Horses running on
fescue prairie at
the Ya Ha Tinda.

PHOTO BY KEN PIGEON.

Warm fall day on
the Ya Ha Tinda.

PHOTO BY MARIE NYLUND.

Bringing in the horses;
early morning.

PHOTO BY BRADFORD WHITE.

FOR SALE

by Canadian Park Service

10,000 ACRES OF CANADA'S FINEST WILDLIFE HABITAT

formerly part of

BANFF NATIONAL PARK

The Ya-Ha-Tinda Ranch is winter home to 1000 elk. Most spend the rest of the year in Banff National Park.

Now the Province of Alberta wants to grab it!

CHAPTER 3
AN UNCERTAIN FUTURE

*FOR SALE: The Ya Ha Tinda Ranch is winter home to 1000 elk. Most spend the rest of
the year in Banff National Park. Now the Province of Alberta wants to grab it!*
—Luigi Morgantini, "The Ya Ha Tinda: An Ecological Overview"

The Murphys might have stayed longer at the Ya Ha Tinda than the (almost) 20 years they did, but it was never quite the same after the poaching incident in 1944. Cliff Murphy no longer had the absolute authority he had taken for granted, and it was not long before the divisiveness and uncertainty over the ranch's status took a toll on the pleasure they had in living there (even though the ranch remained central to the warden patrol network until the end of the Second World War). Also, the Murphys adopted a child and felt they needed to live nearer to other families for schooling. The ranch would never again experience this long period of calm. The Ya Ha Tinda could no longer be ignored. Even during the Murphy years, the federal Department of the Interior had unending debates with Alberta to transfer jurisdiction of natural resources to the province. One of the impediments to this was not having a proper survey of the park boundary restricting where the province could exploit its resources.

As uncertainty over the true boundaries of the Ya Ha Tinda came under increasing scrutiny, its survival as a government horse ranch was threatened by multiple land use proposals. The list included special quarters for high-ranking government officials, a Boy Scout camp, a golf course development, motel/lodge development and a paved highway from the town of Red Deer through to Lake Louise via the Red Deer River. The province had relentlessly sought to obtain the land for its resources, creating rumours that the Ya Ha Tinda was for sale. At one point, Olds College wanted to lease

Ya Ha Tinda
"For Sale" sign.

it as an adjunct to the college's horse program. Unfortunately, the federal government had not always been a great defender for keeping the ranch. Indeed, many officials actively advocated to get rid of it.[71]

After the Murphys left, Banff did not station wardens at the ranch, as it was quite clear it was no longer in the national park. The managing position now became that of foreman. Warden Ernie Young took over from Murphy in 1948, but the following year Lloyd Waekle was hired as foreman. Waekle stayed on in that position for six years (officially designated as "foreman" in 1955) as the upper levels of government tried to sort out the muddled jurisdictional responsibilities. Wrangling and rhetoric did little to clear up whether the federal government had ownership of the surface rights or only the grazing rights. In 1951, things came to a head when a decision was made to have the ranch legally surveyed.[72] It was discovered that somehow the Ya Ha Tinda had been listed in the Alberta Land Titles Office as provincial land under the jurisdiction of the Alberta minister of lands and forests.[73] Officially, the province did not recognize any federal rights at all. By then, a new man, H.G. Jensen, had replaced Huestis as the deputy minister of lands and forests, and relations between the two governments thawed to the point where Jensen actually suggested

the ranch be returned to the park. Taylor notes that Jensen's background was more sympathetic to the park, having served as an Alberta representative on the Eastern Rockies Forest Conservation Board. The board was established in 1947 as a joint federal-provincial agency to manage the provincial forests on the eastern slopes of the Rockies and would become a key player in future decisions surrounding the Ya Ha Tinda.

This momentous offer was ignored, as parks decided it would rather return to an original suggestion of a land exchange whereby the province would gain the Siffleur and Clearwater portions of the park in exchange for additional land around the Ya Ha Tinda. No one could make sense of this and things returned to unresigned limbo. The discovery of oil reserves in the area quickly took the provincial offer off the table.

Perhaps everyone was getting tired of the problematic Ya Ha Tinda. Taylor writes, "The attitude of the deputy minister responsible for national parks [A.J. Hutchison] was so negative that he questioned whether the ranch was a viable operation."[74] His suggestion that it might be better to board the horses instead showed little understanding of the problems that would create. But the chief park warden in Banff knew how vital it was to keep the ranch as a

source of horses for the warden service duties and convinced senior management that it was cost-effective.

Throughout all this, improvements were slowly being undertaken at the ranch. Banff National Park was still responsible for administering the ranch and was the principal source of funding for ranch maintenance. A new barn was built in 1942 and a small bunkhouse and blacksmith shop were completed in 1946.

Different cowboys with backcountry and horse experience, some of who went on to join the warden service, now looked after the ranch. Rumours may have reached the ranch hands from time to time about the political problems, but many things were uncertain during those years, and, for the most part, they kept their heads down and dealt with the daily concerns of running the ranch. Clarence Long – known as "Cougar" Long – was one of the more colourful men who worked there intermittently over a period of five years. Since daily records were not kept (or may have been lost) during these years, accurate dates of occupation cannot be confirmed. Cougar Long was basically a trapper who had come to know the Murphys when he spent the winter there with Dewy Browning in the 1940s. He was a good hand to have around for fencing, breaking horses and haying. Bill Johnson, another bachelor, was

hired on for the same activities. None of these men were involved with patrolling the back-country or law enforcement, departing from what Cliff Murphy would have considered an essential part of his job.

Neil Woledge, who later was a chief park warden of the Kootenay, Yoho and St. Lawrence Island national parks, had worked part-time for the Murphys in 1940 and returned again in 1947–1948. Ernie Young and Neil Woledge both worked there in 1948, but it is unclear what Woledge's position was. He brought his wife and family with him in 1947. He also had the unenviable experience (more so his wife) of having one of his sons born en route to the hospital from the ranch. Not much is documented about this event, but the circumstances speak for themselves. Woledge joined the warden service in Banff after he left the ranch, when a position opened up in 1953. Lloyd Waekle worked at the Ya Ha Tinda year-round and assumed the daily running of the ranch. As such, Woledge would have taken direction from Waekle. Though the wardens continued to treat the Ya Ha Tinda as a base of operations for obtaining horses and as a route through the province to other districts, the main facility was actually too far from the park boundary to base daily patrols out of. A house was finally skidded into the junction of Indianhead Creek and Clearwater River to provide better housing for the district headquarters of the Clearwater River District.

One of the more significant changes to life on the ranch came with the arrival of the Dixon family in 1954 – though it may not have seemed so at the time. Fred Dixon started at the ranch shortly before his family was able to join him. His wife Anne casually stated he was basically "a one-man crew sent out to help foreman Lloyd Waekle."[75] Dixon's real ambition was to join the warden service, which eventually happened in 1957, when he was offered a position at Saskatchewan River Crossing in Banff. The following year, Dixon and Waekle shared the title of foreman, though Waekle had seniority.

It had been many years since a family stayed year-round at the ranch, and the only woman to do so for any length of time prior to that was Nellie Murphy. It seems that the best accounts of life on the ranch came from the women who lived there. Maybe they had more time to keep a journal, or, more likely, they recognized the unique life the ranch had to offer and cherished the time they spent there.

Dixon met his family in Sundre and left on the return trip on a day when the weather was murderous, making it a harrowing drive in. They stayed the first night at the Red Deer River ranger station, halfway between the ranch and Sundre, but faced the same rotten conditions the following morning. Eleanor and Maurice Verhegge, the resident forest ranger and his wife, were their nearest neighbours, and they became close friends, even though they only saw them on trips in and out of town or when the Verhegges made a visit to the ranch.

The sense of isolation and trepidation over their new home dissipated for Anne when the weather cleared and the sun shone on the old log ranch house. Before her lay the beauty of the rolling grass hills, prompting Anne to write, "Distant majestic mountains – a breathtaking view for people like us who were raised on the prairie. It was beautiful but it was an isolated wilderness far from the outside world."[76] The Dixons must have had some pioneer stock in them, as they happily adapted to the isolation and work at the ranch. Their two young girls marked the first time children were raised at the ranch. The extent of their isolation was really noticed when Anne realized the girls became quite shy and would hide under the porch on the rare occasion anyone came to visit.

With this introduction, they began their life at the Ya Ha Tinda. Waekle stayed in the small log bunkhouse, as would other men who came to help with the yearly roundup and shoeing, haying and trailing of horses to the park in the spring. A new workload was added to managing

the ranch when the park decided to increase the cultivation of the hay crop. The Murphys had actually cultivated small sections of hay in the 1930s and 1940s. A group of scientists was sent in from the Department of Agriculture to test various grass species to increase the production of forage crops. This meant clearing and breaking the land for planting in the spring and harvesting in the fall. Through much of the 1950s, the park was wintering, on average, 150 head of horses. The park was also finishing the Cascade Fire Road that went as far as Windy Cabin from Banff. This aided in trailing the horses in the spring and fall, now coming from Yoho, Glacier and Kootenay, as well as Banff.

The need for more hay resulted from the increase in horse use but was almost defeated by a sudden explosion in the elk population. Elk would eventually become a dominant force in the ranch's future, as various interest groups quarrelled over their fate. The culling that had begun in the 1940s had little impact and they continued to increase in numbers at an alarming rate.

Elk have an interesting history in the Rockies of western Canada and the United States, and particularly at the Ya Ha Tinda. Throughout time, the mild weather and low snow accumulation, combined with the rich fescue grass forage, have made the ranch a particularly important range for elk. In addition to this, its isolation meant that for many years the elk were protected from hunting. More significantly, wolves and other natural predators were hunted extensively in the province, which actively sponsored a wolf extermination program. Wolves were also kept under control in the national parks, and their presence in Banff and the Ya Ha Tinda was nonexistent. But elk have also had an erratic history of survival here. The journals of the early explorers, such as David Thompson and Alexander Henry, show that in the early 1800s, elk, similar to bison, became increasingly rare as the traders travelled through the foothills into the mountains. Although elk were hunted throughout the prairies and were periodically found on the Kootenay plains along the Saskatchewan River, they were not even seen in most mountain locations. Bighorn sheep were certainly more abundant. This already low number of elk seems to have further declined in the late 1800s. Luigi Morgantini compiled the historic evidence of elk populations in his ecological overview of the Ya Ha Tinda. He states, "All of the evidence indicate that by the late 1800's and early 1900's, due to a combination of severe winters and indiscriminate hunting by white men and natives, elk had almost disappeared from the Canadian Rocky Mountains."[77] Only a

Haying at the ranch.

remnant herd could be found along the Brazeau River, with a few in the Oldman and Highwood river drainages. It was these low numbers that alarmed Harkin when the park was expanded in 1902. This prompted reintroducing elk from Yellowstone National Park from 1917 to 1920. These animals interbred with the small herds that remained.

By the 1930s, elk were common in Banff National Park, and, by the 1940s, they were starting to be seen in the Panther River and at the Ya Ha Tinda. These numbers, however, were low (50–60 bulls; 80–100 cows) compared to what they would become later. By the time the Dixons arrived, the numbers were increasing, but reports on the population of resident animals varied widely. Numbers from 400 to 1,000 were observed on different occasions. Aerial surveys that flew from 1953 to 1961 gave counts ranging between 516 and 633 head. This may not be the most accurate way to assess actual populations, but it does indicate a consistency that might lead researchers to suspect a true larger population of 1,000. These numbers varied, despite the suspicion that elk numbers were growing. In 1961, R. Webb stated, "Some of the estimates were 'highly colored.'"[78] The movement of elk from valley to valley affected these counts at the Ya Ha Tinda. Elk are migratory by nature and much of the research on their movement had not been studied. Despite the differences in various elk counts, Morgantini stated, "During the 1950's and early 1960's, reports on the size of the elk population that wintered in the Ya Ha Tinda area ranged widely."[79]

Despite the growing concern over the elk populations and the added work of providing hay for the horses, the Dixons quickly settled into life at the ranch. Wes Gilstorf joined the crew in 1955 as a second assistant ranch hand, which helped out greatly. Anne writes, "The life at the Ya Ha Tinda was fantastic."[80] They were too busy to be bothered by the continued debate over the status of the ranch. In fact, it was not formally designated as a horse ranch for the federal government until 1957. This did not affect the daily chores or seasonal work rhythms set out by the custodians of years gone by. For Anne, the isolation was mitigated by the daily running of the ranch, looking after the children and the cooking and cleaning, none of which was lightened by having to haul water and heat everything on a wood stove. The Ya Ha Tinda was run very similarly to western Alberta ranches at the turn of the century. Hot water was a precious commodity, laboriously obtained for multiple tasks. The galvanized washtub was used once a week for the family bath, after which the cooling water was used to wash the floor.

Slim Haugen.

Anne became expert at feeding her family in the typical farm tradition. They had flour from which she baked wonderful light loaves of bread. Due to the high altitude and cold nights, she did not attempt a garden that would produce little to nothing, so vegetables came canned from the store. They did have chickens that supplied both meat and eggs. They got wild meat that she canned and turned into delicious stews. When the men showed up for the shoeing and roundup, she followed tradition and cooked for them as well. She was very surprised to be paid for this, even if it was only a dollar a meal (for up to ten men).

Because the road from Sundre was so bad, the only highlight for company revolved around ranch activity. There were not very many local visitors. After a long winter, with little relief from their own company, the big event of the year was the spring roundup. This was a delight for Anne and possibly for the girls once they got over their shyness. Slim Haugen was a tall quiet wrangler who came to the ranch to shoe horses before they were trailed to the

The Dixons and wranglers at the Ya Ha Tinda sign.

COURTESY FRED AND ANN DIXON FAMILY COLLECTION.

park. Anne always enjoyed his company, with his subtle humour spiced occasionally by his penchant for rum laced with honey. They never forgot to include honey in the spring grocery list. Haugen must have felt she was underpaid when he handed her an extra five-dollar bill, which he placed in her apron pocket, and, with a nod, rode off to join the boys as they galloped behind the park horses heading for Windy Cabin. She felt like a millionaire with nowhere to spend her money.

Rounding up the horses and trailing them back to Banff in the spring was a thrill – particularly for the young fellows just starting on. Slim Haugen never forgot his standard antidote for their first rough day. His rum/honey concoction helped alleviate the saddle sores pounded into these greenhorn cowboys as they bounced along, chasing the wildly running horses through the upper meadows of the Ya Ha Tinda and past the West Lakes. Here the horses often broke, trying for a final escape back to the winter range. Two days and 80 miles later, there was another exhilarating stampede across the wide-open Banff airstrip into the park warden pasture. This would be the ponies' last free run before heading for the different parks for their summer work. Once there, the wardens would be given their horses to travel the backcountry districts for the next six months. The bond they formed with these reliable animals allowed them to become an effective team for the lonely work of keeping their district in top shape.

Both Anne and her family were sad to see the horses go, but it freed them up to enjoy the summer on the ranch. Anne was a keen wildlife observer and kept track of anything wandering through the yard or what she saw on their excursions either on foot or horseback. She notes they saw a lot of black bears but not many grizzlies. Deer were plentiful, as were bighorn sheep, often seen feeding or resting on the high open slopes above the ranch. The wolves that hunted them were not often seen, as they stayed in the high country to hunt the sheep. She saw moose and elk on a regular basis but not in high numbers. It seemed balanced to her.

The second major event of the year for the family occurred in the fall, when the horses were brought back to the ranch. The horses from Kootenay, Yoho and Glacier were trucked to Banff and trailed back to the Ya Ha Tinda over the Cascade and Snow Creek Summit to Scotch Camp and then to the ranch following the new fire road. The shoes would be pulled for the winter and the horses turned out. It was a last chance for wardens and ranch hands to visit before fall turned into winter. It marked a return to winter work and the quiet isolation of that season. For the energetic Dixons, the first priority was getting in the winter's supply of wood. Anne writes, "Wood was our only fuel supply."[81] The ranch hands needed good sleighing conditions to get back into the bush, where the big dead trees were cut and skidded to the ranch. The logs would be cut and stacked behind the old log barn to dry. The stack was eventually sawed and split into cook stove wood, with larger logs being left for the main wood heater.

It was the stove that finally caught the Dixons off guard. Work was so ever-present that they overlooked the amount of wood that was being burnt in the stove. The creosote had been building in the chimney from the time they had been there, and they had no idea when it had last been cleaned. This would eventually lead to a chimney fire when the condensed tar heated to burning temperature. It would go off like a bomb, throwing flames into the air and raining embers down on the roof. The fire that Anne encountered suddenly erupted from the chimney on a hot summer day. Her first reaction was to make sure no one was inside. Next, she saved what was important. Her sewing machine and personal belongings were top priority, and she rescued what she could. When Fred saw the flames and cinders caroming out of the chimney, his immediate concern was that the sparks would start a forest fire if they were caught in

tinder dry trees near the house. Fortunately, the fire blew out on its own and nothing else was damaged. But it did serve to remind them of where they lived and the consequence of not watching everything with a careful eye.

Fred Dixon's real joy at the ranch was the horses. Though the colts were a delight, with the promise of being a true helpmate to some young warden, the older horses with a lifetime of service were his favourites. The children, Connie and Peggy, had their favourite horses as well – they were so quiet, they made excellent playmates that kept the girls safely riding around the ranch for hours on end. But the busy minds in Ottawa were always challenged in justifying their desk jobs. One person was charged with cost cutting and had little idea of what horses were used for anyway. The only thing he could think of was a leather belt. He reasoned it was more practical to kill off the older horses and get some use out of the hides, rather than to waste hay on them. Dixon got a call from headquarters, telling him to kill and skin all horses over 22 years old. Some of these horses still had a lot of useful years left in them. Glen Fagan was sent over from Indianhead to help with this gruesome task. It was the hardest thing either of them had ever done. It was bad enough to shoot these old friends, but skinning them out was terrible. Anne writes, "The hides were taken to Banff but when they got them tanned and ready for use, they couldn't use them. The hides were too thin … it was really hard on Fred, really hard."[82]

But the work of running the ranch continued, although it would never erase that miserable burden. Haying was becoming a priority, and, when the barn loft was full, it became a cozy bed for the wardens coming in for the spring roundup or retuning the horses in the fall for the winter. The empty bottles of whisky buried in the hay were certain proof that everyone slept well.

Life on the ranch was never really dull with the work and the encounters with wildlife. Bears were prevalent at the ranch and often a nuisance. A scrappy cat seemed the best defense against the black intruders whenever they approached the animal's porch domain. The biggest challenge was the long dark hours of winter. They had only been there one winter when Lloyd Waekle was informed that at the age of 65 he could no longer be employed by the government. He was mandatorily retired – a strict government policy at the time. Waekle was not ready for this and hated to go. Dixon was summarily made foreman, though it seemed like he was stepping into shoes that did not belong to him.

Jack Schulte, a ranch hand who had been sent out from Banff to help with winter projects, alleviated the tedium of their first winter in 1955. Schulte's uncle had a dog team up north, so he had some experience with training them. It was the Banff park superintendent, however, who capitalized on these skills. He had a wandering old dog with one bad eye that was repeatedly picked up and put in the pound by the wardens. When he got tired of constantly retrieving his dog, he asked Schulte to give him a home at the ranch. Other dogs showed up and Schulte decided to make harnesses and see if they could be turned into a dog team. This became the winter project that kept them entertained for some time. A white Samoyed that had seven pups helped the team along. They were put to work as soon as they were old enough to be trained to shoulder a harness and pull a sled.

Though the Dixons only spent a few years years at the Ya Ha Tinda, they were memorable. Before Fred Dixon was offered a permanent warden position at Saskatchewan River Crossing, he had a chance to work with Cal Hayes, who would eventually become the ranch foreman in the years to come. Before Hayes became foreman, however, Mickey Gilmar took over for Dixon. Gilmar actually worked with Earl Hayes, Donald Sutherland, Jim Quinn and Charley Weatherlee. He was raised in the

Crow's Nest Pass in southern Alberta, along with his brother Larry Gilmar who would eventually become a warden in Banff. Gilmar's wife Evelyn, who he married at the tender age of 16, found life on the ranch more difficult than some of the previous ranch wives. It was a major adjustment to a male-dominant environment, considering she was quite an independent spirit. They moved there in 1958 with two young girls and had a third while living there.

One of the biggest benefits was getting a new house. The old log house had served its purpose and was in such disrepair it was deemed time to build a new one. G.H.L. (Harry) Dempster was the superintendent in Banff, and he began to take a special interest in the ranch. It seems he had some arguments on his hands from headquarters personnel, who could not understand why a simple bunkhouse would not provide all that was needed. This blind spot was quickly overcome, and Evelyn Gilmar was even given some say in how the kitchen should be designed to feed the spring and fall crews. What resulted was a much larger, three-bedroom, spacious house that is still used today. Evelyn was expected to put on big meals when work crews showed up, and the new kitchen made the work much more manageable. But Evelyn had more modern ideas than her predecessors and wanted equal pay for equal work.

The dollar per meal seemed a bit short-changed to her – particularly for a woman who wanted to make her own way in the world.[83]

One of the ranch hands who worked for Mickey Gilmar was Lorne Cripps, who was joined by his wife Shirley. He had had an eclectic career as a logger, packer, farrier, power-saw mechanic and camp cook, which was the sort of background appreciated at the Ya Ha Tinda. Though the Cripps were only at the ranch a short while, from 1957 to 1959, they loved the time they spent there. Shirley said, "I loved being able to ride with Lorne almost every day. It was a wonderful winter. The ranch was beautiful all winter especially with all the elk."[84]

On one occasion, Cripps rode as far as Indian Head Cabin with Smokey Guttman, who would become the resident warden for the Clearwater River District. Guttman brought his young wife Vin along for company and to help with the chores for the summer season. Though she was comfortable with horses and the outdoors, this would be her first experience living in an isolated location for several months in the remote district. The trip over the pass was anything but encouraging. It was still choked with snow, and they hardly made it over the summit. Cripps recalled, "We left them at Indianhead and headed back toward the ranch. As we rode away, Vin kept waving to us and kept waving as long as she could still see us. I saw her in Whitehorse years later and I said, 'I sure felt sorry for you that day.' Vin replied, 'It probably wasn't half as bad as I felt for myself!'"[85]

The two years the Cripps spent on the ranch were a highlight in Lorne's and Shirley's lives. Shirley loved riding out to see the elk, which on one occasion "thought we were trying to cut them off, so they stopped, turned back and went across in front of us again. It was amazing how they tried to outguess us."[86] Cripps reported seeing up to 1,000 head of elk at one time, as well as numerous bighorn sheep and the odd moose. Elk were still enigmatic in their movements as far as the cowboys were concerned – one day there would be large herds on the range that would suddenly be gone the next day. When the elk finally did move out, Cripps reported seeing cougar numbers increase, attracted by sheep that were now more numerous around the ranch. The alarming number of cougars on the ranch became enough of a concern that they hired Clarence Long from Sundre to hunt what he could. That winter, he killed 13 cougars.

When the Cripps were there, the ranch was wintering 200–250 head of horses, depending on the year, which was close to the maximum kept there at any one time. The colts were trained by the ranch hands for both packing and riding but were still newly broke when the wardens picked them up in the spring. The ranch hands were good enough to accompany the wardens as far as Scotch Camp, where they picked up their string, to give them a better understanding of the horses they would be working with. The big horse drives to Banff were coming to an end with the completion of the Cascade Fire Road directly linking Banff to the Ya Ha Tinda. Now the various park horses could be trucked back to their respective summer residences.

As wonderful as life could be at the ranch, it was most rewarding for the men. It probably took a harder toll on the women, who were more confined to the house and the daily chores of cooking and cleaning. Shirley Cripps had been a teacher and by spring she was eager to get back to it. Lorne Cripps had the opportunity to become a warden, but that would mean living in a warden district year-round. Though it suited him, he later mentioned, "I was used to the quiet and I loved it but by spring Shirley wanted to get back to teaching." The compromise was a ranch at Winfield, where they spent the rest of their lives.[87]

Another interesting jack of all trades who went to work on the ranch in 1958 was Don Brestler. He grew up at Twin Butte, south of Pincher Creek, where he worked as a cowboy and packer for Andy Russell, but it was working at the ranch that he refers to as an experience he would not forget, writing, "It had been a great summer and it had provided a fond memory that I will treasure forever!"[88] He was working in Calgary when he met Bob Hand, then chief park warden in Banff. Hand had been looking for an individual who was good with horses to work at the Ya Ha Tinda and offered the job to Brestler. His answer was immediate: "I couldn't say 'yes' quick enough."[89] A few days later, he made the long drive to the ranch, and reported to his new boss, Mickey Gilmar. He was exhausted when the welcome pillows of the small bunkhouse finally hit his head. Because he had arrived at dusk, the view from his window the following morning was his first impression of the world he would come to know well. Gilmar drove him around to familiarize him with the country, which he found spectacular beyond anything he had expected. Beyond the outstanding setting, he was impressed with the abundance of wildlife. In the yard, the resident dogs and six bighorn sheep standing by the big wooden front gate greeted him. Horses dotted the landscape, mingling with a sizable herd of elk. A richness and peace pervaded this place, with its comforting protective mountains that sent storms into the atmosphere. The only winds allowed into this protected enclave were the gentle warming Chinook winds that kept the place warm and dry.

Brestler started with eight, three-year-old colts to break for riding and packing. Gilmar gave him space to work the colts at his own pace in the corral until they were ready to face the grim reality of creeks, the bush, rivers, bogs and wildlife encounters. His favourite ride was the trail to Clearwater Summit, ten miles return. The colts would encounter all they had to deal with when finally sent out on the trail to the backcountry district they would be assigned to. He noted, "Only about half of them bucked me off."[90]

Throughout the summer and fall, Brestler fell into the rhythm of the ranch. He learned to pack horses, throw the diamond hitch and enjoy the rewards of backcountry trips to outlaying warden cabins. The summer passed into autumn and the freshness of cool mornings turned the trees to their spectacular fall colours. The evenings were brought to song by the bugling of bull elk rounding up their herd for the winter. Ponds began to form a skin of new ice, heralding the season to come.

Brestler was a gifted artist and writer. He was also open about his experiences on the ranch and was able to put into written words what most people who live there feel but cannot say. It was the following summer when he made an

obligatory trip to Calgary to visit his grandfather who had come down with cancer that the impact of his time spent on the Ya Ha Tinda accosted him. The contrast stunned him:

> It was Stampede week in Calgary and the place was buzzing. There were girls, stores, transit buses, traffic lights and vehicles. It all seemed so strange and overwhelming to me. I didn't feel a part of it anymore. I had the strongest urge to turn around head back for the ranch and never come out again. I was bushed! It's almost indescribable. I had heard about it but never thought it would happen to me.[91]

Bighorn sheep in the front yard.

CHAPTER 4
SOME DEGREE OF SETTLEMENT

The ranch was almost mythically seen as the heritage and heart of the
warden service. They were not going to lose it without a fight.
—Kathy Calvert

When the Dixons left in 1957, there was an indication on the horizon of a permanent settlement of the legal status of the Ya Ha Tinda. The original order-in-council of 1930 recognized the Ya Ha Tinda was land ceded to the federal government as a federal reserve within a provincial forest reserve, but it left unresolved issues never really accepted by the provincial government. In 1952, Deputy Minister of Lands and Forests H.G. Jensen recognized the concerns over jurisdiction that had cropped up over the years between the two governments and tried to resolve the problem. This only caused parks to dust off old negotiations of land swaps that no one was interested in and, after two years, the issue was still not resolved. Oil discovered on the ranch only solidified the determination of the province to fight for rights

to the land. A new deputy minister in Ottawa wanted to get rid of the ranch altogether but was fought tooth and nail by Banff National Park, supported by a number of national parks in Alberta and British Columbia. They won the argument that the most cost-effective way of supplying horses to the park service was by keeping the Ya Ha Tinda, and once again the land was set aside for grazing rights for the federal government.

On February 7, 1958, by a second order-in-council, the province granted 9,750 acres to Canada in accordance with the 1930 Natural Resources Act, less the mineral rights.[92] This time, the boundaries were formally surveyed. The Ya Ha Tinda was now in the federal government's domain and it was only theirs to lose. With jurisdiction finally resolved, long-term

Peppi Stepper's
first colt.

management plans were put in place. The plans included expanding the hay cultivation, fencing and developing a formal breeding program. The future looked good, with no lack of work ahead.

By far, the expansion of the horse-breeding program was the most exciting part of the long-range plans. A breeding program had already been established, with records going back as far as 1938, but it had no formal agenda, with the studs coming from an eclectic stock. Georgina Campbell wrote an article for the *Canadian Horse Journal*, documenting some of this history: "Over the years almost every breed of stallion has been used, including a grade Belgian, a Thoroughbred Hunter, a Clydesdale and even a wild mustang."[93] Mickey Gilmar talked the park into providing better breeding stock, and the first registered stallion was Peppi Stepper, a registered quarter horse. All of the horses have the sheep head brand, in addition to a foot brand indicating the year of birth and the name of the horse.

Along with more horses being kept at the ranch, grazing permits issued to outfitters increased the number of horses wintering in the area. Though these grazing rights were not on the ranch proper, they impacted the total forage available on the eastern slopes of Banff National Park [94]

The competition for this range was greatly exacerbated in the 1940s, when, aided by ongoing predator control of wolves and cougars, the reintroduced elk began to thrive alarmingly well in their historic habitat. In 1944, Bob Hand, later the chief park warden in Banff, and a firm proponent of maintaining or increasing the horse stock at the ranch, was so concerned he recommended wholesale slaughter of the elk on the Ya Ha Tinda. The ranch – to the dismay of Nellie Murphy – was opened up for a large-scale hunt as early as 1940. She recalls, "Truckloads of hunters descended on the ranch."[95] She had no idea how many elk were actually taken, but in her opinion it was not going to have a lasting effect. Interestingly, Hand's preference for horse use at the Ya Ha Tinda was in direct opposition to the opinion of former Chief Park Warden Bruce Mitchell, who did not think the ranch was worth keeping at all. In 1944, he wrote a memorandum to the Department of the Interior entitled, "Suggested Improvements in the Warden Service Organization." In it he states, "Due to the inaccessibility of the Ya Ha Tinda Ranch and the expenditure required to build a new house, corrals etc., I would recommend that the department sell the property which I would value at approximately $25,000.00. I

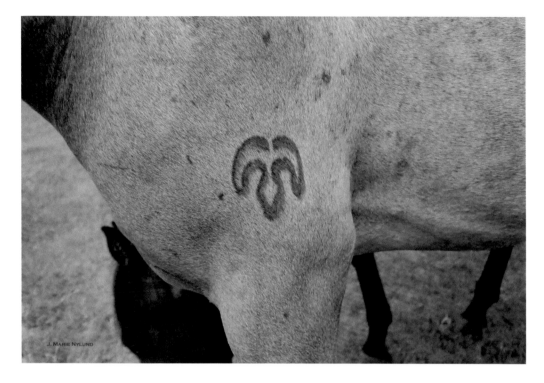

Ya Ha Tinda sheep
head horse brand.

COURTESY JOHN AND MARIE
NYLUND COLLECTION.

would then suggest that this Department purchase some land in the vicinity of Cochrane, which would be developed into the future government ranch."[96] It was not just the conflict between horse and elk that continued to be a problem for the Ya Ha Tinda but also its isolated location. Yet the location was never a problem for the warden service, which treasured the ranch as the foundation of its operations in the guardianship of the national parks.

When the Gilmars arrived at the Ya Ha Tinda, the elk population was still on the ascendency. But the knee-jerk reaction of simply shooting them was now being thought out a bit more carefully. The park decided to take a more scientific approach to the problem and, in 1961, the Canadian Wildlife Service assigned biologist Don Flook to give it a more informed opinion about forage use by elk and horses.[97] The research started with a simple transect approach to study the forage, with the reasoning that horses and elk might rely on different plant species as a food source and not be in as much conflict as originally thought.

R. Webb, a second biologist who was also studying the problem, was a bit quicker to conclude there was indeed a problem. He may have been a bit more biased, however, as he reported directly to Alberta Fish and Wildlife, which still harboured wishful thoughts of having the land eventually returned to the province. It wanted a say in the use of the ranch, which it felt could only support one large grazing species. Suddenly, there was a concern that horses competed too successfully with the elk. The province wanted an environment that sustained large elk herds that would ultimately become a source of revenue through hunting. Webb found the native grass in poor condition and recommended another heavy cull of elk, with restrictions placed on the number of horses that could be wintered on the ranch. The elk cull went ahead, with the hope of preventing further erosion and helping the fescue grass recover from overgrazing. Though this recommendation did not result in the loss of the number of horses kept at the ranch, the culling would go on for some years.[98]

The success in reducing the number of elk might be what spurred former Banff Superintendent Dempster, now assigned regional supervisor, to recommend that Jasper horses be brought into the Ya Ha Tinda program.[99] Jasper National Park had always looked after its own horses, as it was too far to trail them through the mountains from the ranch to the Maligne Range in Jasper. Trucking had its own problems, as it was a long drive over the Icefields Parkway, then up the rough road to the ranch from Banff. The park chose instead to winter its horses at another lush, open, montane valley called Willow Creek, a backcountry district north and east of the Jasper townsite. Some of the horses were also kept on the Maligne Range for winter use. In 1962, Jasper was given the opportunity to winter its horses at Elk Island National Park, which suited the park to a tee, as the trucking distance was short and on good roads. Mac Elder was a warden in Jasper at the time and recalls the horses always coming back in the best shape he had ever seen them.

Therefore, it came as an unpleasant surprise when Jasper was suddenly told to winter its horses at the Ya Ha Tinda. At the time, Jasper had almost half the complement of horses in the mountain parks. At one time it was using 90 head of horses. Trucking the horses to the Ya Ha Tinda in the 1960s was an onerous task. Elder thought the change had to do with the pressure being put on the government by the North American Elk Foundation, which wanted the horses removed altogether. The foundation, according to Elder, "was pretty much financed and managed with American money. It was pretty big in the U.S. They had some influence at the time in trying to get the horses out of there."[100]

Mac Elder had reason to be concerned about the switch. Mickey McGuire was chief park warden in Jasper at the time and supervised the switch to trucking the horses to the Ya Ha Tinda rather than to Elk Island National Park. However, McGuire "was very opposed to it." Elder recalls, "The trucking was very hard on those horses, and we weren't happy about what was going on." To illustrate his point, Elder described a particularly difficult trip one fall bringing the horses back to the Ya Ha Tinda after a full summer's work in the mountains. It took two days to get the horses to the ranch, as they had to be driven to Banff, where they spent the night on the local horse range. But from there it was a very long day up the roughly built Cascade Fire Road over Snow Creek Summit and down via the Scotch Camp warden cabin to the ranch. Elder describes it this way: "Well, those poor horses – after two days of trucking in there they were just all done in when they arrived. They would stand around for two or three days before they would eat; they were so

tired. They would hold up one foot and then they would hold up the other foot. They wandered around but it was rough on them."[101]

In 1974, the road between Sundre and Mountainaire Lodge was built to the standard that could handle large truck liners, allowing a greater number of horses to be trucked in one load. However, the only paved section was between Jasper and Edmonton. The liner was not on pavement for long. Once it hit Edson, the route went south on a gravel road to Rocky Mountain House and Sundre, where the trucker turned west on the new road to Mountainaire Lodge. The gravel section, covering a distance of 455 km, was composed of rough gravel and crushed rocks, which was very hard on tires. From Mountainaire Lodge to the ranch, the horses were transported in much smaller trucks to handle the narrow winding road. On one occasion, the trucker hired to drive the horses back in the spring was unprepared for the rough conditions and kept getting flat tires, prolonging the time the horses had to remain in the truck. Elder recalled this event in an interview, saying, "The driver phoned around four-thirty in the morning. He said he was down at the service station on the east side of Jasper townsite. He was there and he had a load of horses. He had hauled them over that gravel road. He told me that he had three or four flat tires on his rig. Then he said, 'I don't know what I'm going to do. I have had these horses in this truck since yesterday.'[102] Elder came down to help the driver unload them, but he must have wondered if they would recover after such a prolonged and stressful trip. During the first two years of wintering the horses at the ranch, they came back in such poor condition that many could not be used until they recovered on the Maligne Range in Jasper.

The hilly, windy, gravel road was never good in the off-seasons (spring or fall), and it could turn nasty in a matter of hours if a snowstorm moved in. The truck driver hired to bring the horses back to Jasper in the spring of 1995 was not familiar with the route from Mountainaire Lodge to Sundre. He missed the turnoff to Sundre and proceeded north toward the small hamlet of Bearberry. The weather was poor and before he reached the town he encountered icy conditions going up a steep switchback hill. The truck brakes failed to stop him when he spun out on a curve, causing the outfit to slide backwards over a bank and tip over. The end result was the loss of 17 head of horses. Slim Haugen was contacted at the ranch to attend the scene with a rifle. He was forced to shoot 17 horses that were hurt beyond recovery.[103] It was a bad year for the Jasper horse population, as many more picked up swamp fever while wintering

with horses from another park. In total, Jasper lost 70 head that year, which had to be replaced by horses bought at auctions. Horses sold at auction are an unknown quantity, and there was no guarantee they would be suitable for work in the mountains. It took years to replace those horses from the brood stock supplied by the ranch.

In 1960 Chief Park Warden Dempster was promoted to administer the newly created Western Regional Office as regional supervisor – a sudden addition to parks administration.[104] By 1970, the Western Regional Office began to take over the major planning for the ranch, as well as the operational budget. Park Warden Don Mickle, also cultural resource manager for Banff, Lake Louise, Kootenay and Yoho, wrote in a short paper on the Ya Ha Tinda that the regional office was "apparently providing central direction in so far as policy and standardization of the horse program were concerned and Banff still contributing many of the resources. According to this understanding Banff's Chief Park Warden, Bert Pittaway and Resource Conservation Officer Jim Sime would represent respectively the park and the region in the operation of the ranch."[105]

Due to Dempsters' long tenure in Banff, the interest in the welfare of the ranch did not waiver. For the staff at the ranch, life continued as before, with some peace of mind knowing the new situation was not about to bring drastic changes. Much of the political maneuvering swirled above them in a foreign dialogue captured in the stratosphere where it stayed, not affecting the daily work routine on the ground.

As with previous decades, the spring was the most exciting time of the year for winter-weary ranch residents. The colts heading to the various parks for the first time received their final training before leaving the ranch. Park horse farriers Slim Haugen and Jack Rae had to shoe all the horses – a huge job in itself – and hay fallowing was begun and winter-ravaged fences had to be repaired. And, of course, they had to bring in the unbroken young horses to start their first horse school. They were also getting an onslaught of biologists and archaeologists ready to study everything that moved or did not move. Evelyn Gilmar worked long hours feeding people as they came and went while trying to run a household and manage her children. After the loneliness of the winter, the place must have seemed like a circus with so many people coming and going.

It was also spring roundup time for the outfitters, who wintered their horses just south of the Red Deer River. Not only was there a lot of activity at the ranch but the outfitters

Working with horses in the corral.

COURTESY ANN DIXON COLLECTION.

would also make the place seem even busier as they searched and chased horses throughout the latter part of May and early June. They had individual camps near the Ya Ha Tinda boundary, close to the present-day Bighorn Campground just outside the main gate to the ranch. It was an exciting time, with the valley echoing the yell of riders and the thundering of horses as they ran for the winged corrals awaiting their capture. Bert Mickle, a rancher from Millarville, bought the Lake Louise outfit from Ray Legace in 1962 and was one of the outfitters camped there. Don Mickle, who would later become a park warden, is Bert's son and remembers those early roundups with great fondness. Don's vivid account of gathering the horses sheds a small light on the excitement and the dangers:

Cowboy crossing the Red Deer River.

A lot of the horses would be gathered on the high grasslands of the Ribbon Creek Flats. It was important to scout out how many horses were close by and plan a chase in the morning. We required more saddle horses for the next day to mount the rest of the crew. There were only four horses trucked in to start the round up.

Across the main channel of the river was an island with two large round corrals. This was where we would attempt to capture all of the horses in the following days. There was another large corral about twelve miles south on the Panther River at the Corners. A lot of our horses ranged in that area. When we trapped them in the Panther corral we had to trail them twelve miles back to the Red Deer corral.

As the remuda was rounded up, they would be grazed near Eagle Lake on the eastern edge of the Ya Ha Tinda Ranch. The round up crew would take turns herding the captured horses then put them back in the holding corrals at night. It took at least two riders to carefully watch the caught horses so that they wouldn't slip back across the river.

The four riders started across the river, which was rising fast. Ben was a rookie for crossing high water so I rode him next to Dad. He was riding Cinnamon, a tall sorrel mare who had many years of river crossings under her tail. Ben crossed like a pro. Keith [Foster, a local Millarville cowboy] gave a (sort of) compliment by saying "Jesus Mick – I think that ugly shitter of yours has webbed feet."

It wasn't quite swimming water yet but – it was still raining and there was a lot of snow had to melt in the mountains. Keith was riding Pick Pocket; a gritty little bay gelding that was kept at the ranch that

The Mickle roundup, early 1960s.

winter. *Pick Pocket earned his name when one of the guides bent over to shoe his front foot. The agile little bay reached up with his hind foot and ripped off the back pocket of the farrier's jeans.*

We rode up the hill on the wide seismic line, which intersects the pack trail in several places. At the top is an old rail fence, which was used to try and wing horses down the trail through previous decades of horse chasing. The riders approached the edge of the flats and there were about forty horses in various small bands scattered throughout the meadows. It was an exhilarating sight as the setting sun broke through the clouds. There was one band of about a dozen horses close by and some of our choice saddle horses were among them. We decided to try and capture this small bunch while we were there so we would have more saddle horses for an early morning gather. We spread out and carefully worked our way around the unsuspecting herd.

A black shadow emerged from behind a tree. It was one of the old lead mares named Two-bits. Her ears were down and she took off for the thickest timber without hesitation. It seemed like she was waiting for us. "Oh shit – where did that old bitch come from," hollered Keith.

There were a few lead mares that always gave us trouble and made for interesting campfire stories. The most notorious were Two-bits and White Lady. Two-bits was a rangy black mare that was exceptionally crafty. White Lady was a small white mare and a chosen elder of the herd for her cunning ability to give riders the slip.

Two-bits broke into a lope and the rest of the dirty dozen headed off behind her like they were being chased by a pack of wolves. They soon scattered in different directions and so did the riders. Ben and I ended up behind Two-bits and three of her cronies. I could still hear Keith screaming obscenities in the distance. We seemed to be drifting west as we wound our way through the heavy timber and down the steep hill. Ben's brakes were failing again and I hung on and tried to dodge around whatever trees that

we could. A large branch was coming at me at eye level. I ducked my head and waited to be lifted from the saddle but the branch was rotten and broke into a cloud of splinters and I was somehow still in the saddle. We were on an old elk trail that was winding its way down the hill toward the Red Deer River and finally broke out on a steep bank on the edge of the river – about five miles west of our corrals.

I realized that if the horses were forced across the river they could probably be kept under control and we might be able to get these wily steeds back to the corrals. We bolted along the riverbank. Ben was fast enough to keep the horses from doubling back to the darkening forest. Finally one of the horses was tired of the game and skidded down a gully to the river. The other two followed but old Two-bits tried to break along the bank once more. Ben put his ears back and charged her. I tried frantically to pull on the brakes as Ben rammed Two-bits in the shoulder. The three of us went over the bank into the Red. I felt like the guy in the cartoon yelling "Whoa" as he rode over a big cliff. We hit the water with a resounding splash and I managed to stay upright in the saddle as we floated across to the three steeds waiting on the other side. I looked back at the *bank that we had leaped which was about ten feet above the river. I gave Ben a thankful pat on the shoulder. After reaching the north side of the river the fugitives trotted along like the gentle dude and packhorses that they were supposed to be.*[106]

The Gilmars' tenure continued to be uneventful from a political standpoint. Although the regional office provided general direction, as in previous years, most of the issues were solved relatively smoothly by working with the Banff administration through the office of the chief park warden. During those years, Earl Hayes, a cowboy, horse breaker and farrier, was a ranch hand under Gilmar. Aside from the brief time the Cripps and Don Brestler were at the ranch, the two men, plus Gilmar's wife, Evelyn, made up the full complement of staff.

Hayes was offered the job at the Ya Ha Tinda in 1959 after working for the warden service in Banff. He took his young wife Colleen with him, along with boxes of dishes they would have a long time in finding a use for. Colleen remembers, "Off we went with a new wringer washing machine, old bed with a horse hair mattress and many boxes of fine china and crystal. We lived in the little log cabin behind the black smith shop. Mickey and Evelyn Gilmar and the girls were there at the time. When a new house

was built we moved into the old log house and later to the house on the top of the hill. It was a motel unit brought in from Banff."[107]

The Hayes had two children, Larry and Barb, while they lived on the ranch. Constantly aware of how easily they could be stranded, Colleen decided to spend the last months of her pregnancy in Banff, where the babies were born in the hospital. The kids spent their early years at the Ya Ha Tinda, and Colleen amused herself by taking movies of the family and daily events. At that time the road from Banff was built as far as Scotch Camp, where a crew was busy working on the bridge across the Red Deer River. Until it was built, the horses for the parks were trailed to that point, from where they could be trucked to Banff.

They loved living at the ranch, but it was Colleen who documented the impact that hunters had on those working on the ranch. On one return trip from Scotch Camp, they spotted a small abandoned elk calf that they brought back to the ranch. "We kept her in Larry's [their son] bedroom overnight and then put her in the barn with the Gilmar milk cow and her calf. She was tame as she thought she was a calf. Evelyn was making arrangements for her to go to Al Oeming's game farm when a hunter shot her in the pasture in front of the house. She had red on and was even wearing a bell!"[108]

Despite year-round access by road from Sundre, the place was still quite isolated by modern standards, with only the phone line or single-side band radio to connect them to the outside world. The entertainment for most of the year came from a radio or the odd visitor. It was a life that suited those who did not mind the hard work and isolation, but such circumstances can lead to tension for those forced together in such confinement. For Evelyn Gilmar, despite having her children for company, living on the ranch became an increasing hardship. Though she was an excellent cook, she did not appreciate cooking for large crews and anyone else who dropped by. She was particularly incensed that she was not paid for this work. This would change a few years after she arrived, and she eventually was compensated for all her work but at a wage she considered inadequate. Her third pregnancy at the ranch left her feeling desperate, and an accident with a gun that sent both she and the baby to the hospital added to her sense of isolation. Colleen recalls, "Our most frightening experience was when Evelyn accidently shot herself in the barn. She was nine months pregnant. Fortunately a city policeman was in the yard. They got her into the old house and tried to phone for help. Having trouble getting through, Earl raced off to phone from Scotch Camp."[109]

Meanwhile, Colleen boiled water while waiting for help.

The late 1950s and 1960s were not known for sensitivity toward people's ability to adapt to the mental toughness required to handle life year after year on the Ya Ha Tinda. Besides, it was the men that were hired for their ability as ranch hands and horse breakers, not their wives. If they chose to bring their family with them, it was their prerogative, and if the family had problems, it was not a government matter. Wives were certainly not interviewed for the job and had to adapt or leave. Everyone who worked there was thrown into the stew, and it was their business to sort out how they got along. Some stayed happily for years, while others enjoyed it while they were there but moved on once the experience ran its course.

Don Brestler recounts how these tensions built up, and, in his case, led to him leaving the ranch. They were about to get a quarter horse stud for the breeding program, and Mickey Gilmar decided they should build a separate corral to keep him from the brood mares. But first they had to cut the posts. Brestler wrote in his memoirs,

Mickey directed me to a small grove of trees behind the buildings to cut the posts from. They were either crooked or too small, so I cut the best ones I could find. Mickey rode his old red horse up to see how I was doing. He looked at the cut down trees and said nothing. When I dragged them into the yard the next day he came over to look at them. He faced me with an angry look on his face and said "There's not one straight f__ ing post here!" and stomped off. I put down my axe and went to the main house, phoned the Chief Warden and asked for a transfer. I met Mickey in the yard and told him that I quit. He admitted it was a poor selection of trees to choose from and he should have said something when he saw the fallen trees. He was sweet as pie to me after that but it was too late, the damage was done. No wonder that Cal Hayes, the rider before me, only lasted six months. Cal, however, returned later to be foreman of the ranch for the rest of his park service.[110]

In 1965, Don Sutherland became foreman and worked with a variety of ranch hands over the next three years, none of who stayed longer than a couple of summers. The horse-breeding and training program continued to be the main priority of the ranch. The exact way the horses were handled and broken always seemed to ignite a difference of opinion. The attitude toward breaking horses was slowly changing due to the influence of gentler methods filtering up from the United States, employed by men later known as "horse whisperers." But it was not something that caught on rapidly in Canada. Richard Reignier, who worked there for three years from 1967 to 1969, as a foreman and wrangler, had little good to say about how the horses were being turned out. His observation was succinct and to the point: "When I was first there, they had thirty-three head of horses to start. They had a different foreman (not Sutherland) for a couple of years that had a crew of hippies working for him. They just about ruined all the horses."[111]

He does not really specify who the "hippies" were, but it clearly indicates that most wranglers will, at some point, have a disagreement on how a horse should be broken. If a person earns a reputation as having a "good hand" with a horse, it is a high, hard-won compliment.[112]

By 1967, Cal Hayes returned to the ranch as a ranch hand. He worked sporadically at the ranch over the years, leaving periodically to work for the Albert Forest Service and as a supervisor for what was then called the "Native fire crew" in Banff National Park. Then, in 1969, Mickey and Evelyn Gilmar moved to an acreage near Blackfalls, close to Red Deer, where they could enroll their kids in school and Evelyn could finally earn a living wage. Cal Hayes was the obvious choice as the new foreman. He had turned up briefly at the ranch in 1957 to work for Fred Dixon. He came back again in 1963, when Don Sutherland was in charge, and went on to work under Bill Burles for a number of years. Hayes was a small man who always wore a small curl of his hair in the middle of his forehead like a signature beacon – some said just to annoy his wife. He was a man of strong opinions and loyalties. He was rarely indifferent. He either liked you or did not. If he liked you, he was considered the best boss a person could have. Those he did not get along with usually did not stay long.

He always had his "eye on things" at the ranch and did not trust that the public would be respectful.[113] He kept his binoculars on the table so he could see who was coming up the road and would often take a drive through the Bighorn Campground just to see who was there. Lorne Cripps worked on the ranch in 1957 and recalled a story about Hayes's visit to the campground that reveals part of his personality:

The best story I heard about Cal was the time he was doing a check through the camping area. I believe he was a forest officer at the time. A man and woman didn't do things quite right, so Cal gave them a ticket. Years later, this same couple, were

back once again. Cal came along, his parks' Stetson hat pulled down tight. The couple proceeded to tell him about a bad experience they'd had years ago with this miserable ranger who had a distinctive curl on his forehead. Well, Cal with his ever-loving dry sense of humor proceeded to take his hat off and say how sorry he was that they'd had such a poor experience. The couple left that night. I could just see Cal doing this![114]

Don Mickle vividly remembers when he first met Hayes while on a spring roundup.

Every year in early June we would round up our outfitting horses from the Ribbon Creek and the Corners area across the Red Deer River and south of the Ya Ha Tinda Ranch. We brought horses down to our holding corral on the bank of the Red Deer River. One day we brought in a strange older horse that we had no idea where it came from. It was a gnarly old horse and had several different brands on its hide. Dad (Bert Mickle) said we would trail it along and add it to our string. We later did figure out that it might have been from somebody's bucking string when we tried to pack it. Cal Hayes stopped in to visit us at our camp. He took a look at the old horse and said – "By golly Bert – you had better find a

Cal Hayes at the ranch house.

big blanket to cover up all those brands on that old nag"![115]

Hayes's brisk manner came shining through on another occasion Mickle never forgot.

We were on the round up again. Ron Hall, Paul Peyto and I chased a bunch of horses down to our holding corral on the Red Deer River. There were a couple of Erling Strom's horses with our string. We were just heading them into the corral when one of Strom's old packhorses put its ears flat and backed up to kick. I couldn't stop or turn my saddle horse in time and the old packhorse nailed my knee with both hooves. It lifted me off my saddle and I was rolling around on the ground holding my knee while Paul and Ron finished corralling the horses. Just then, Cal Hayes came driving in from the Ya Ha Tinda to see what we were up to. He jumped out of the truck and said – "You boys got those ponies in the corral – good." He pointed at me rolling around holding my knee and said "That boy is hurt – Ron you grab him by the heels and Paul you grab him by the ears and put him in the truck and take him down to Sundre." It turned out to be a chip broken off of my knee – but not a broken leg![116]

Dale Portman, who once worked for Bert Mickle and became a park warden, remembers Cal Hayes with a chuckle: "He had a pecker pot disposition, much like a bantam rooster, always with a mischievous glint in his eye and I always wondered where he was going to direct his gaze next. When I hadn't seen him for a while, the first words out of his mouth were always memorable, if sometimes unquotable. He had an infectious laugh and if he was sitting at the time, it was often accented by a brisk slap to the knee. His sharp wit would soon follow."[117]

Hayes was strict and ran the ranch as if it were his own, with no ambiguity as to what he wanted out of those who worked for him. He was also kind-hearted and particularly loved children. Christine Cripps visited the ranch whenever she could and said, "I loved going into the ranch. I had heard about it from my parents (Lorne and Shirley Cripps) and I knew Cal would always give me a cup of tea, a hard time and his 'look.' He let me take a horse up Scalp Creek for a ride. He and his wife Donna both had a heart of gold. Later on, Donna made the table centrepieces and the top for my wedding cake."[118]

One of the main entertainments for the wardens out on patrol in the park was the morning show on the single-side band radio with Moe Vroom, Cal Hayes and the Banff barn boss, Jim Burles. In 1974, I was one of the first women to be hired on as a warden and had a chance to listen to the "Moe and Cal" show on a fall trip trailing the Yoho horses back to the ranch for the winter. It was my first trip outside the park, and I was a bit nervous about meeting the infamous ranch boss. But there was nothing in the morning show to give cause for concern. After the essential morning radio call was over, the three old friends would gabble on about the gossip in Banff, voicing their opinions on all the comings and goings, dotted by Hayes's colourful phrases as he teased Moe, to which she always had a sharp comeback. It would have been easy to pass half the morning listening to them.

When we got to the ranch with the string of Yoho horses, my first impression of Hayes was a lively outgoing cowboy not much taller than myself. He was very friendly and took great interest in how I was doing on the job. Because we were both short, and usually had to plan on how to deal with tall horses, his first advice was "never give a horse an even break." What he meant was not to worry about what anyone thinks and always use the terrain to your advantage. If a horse is going to buck, it will likely happen if you are struggling to reach the saddle. I took that advice to heart and never worried about anyone's opinion if I sought good ground to mount. To my delight,

Hayes also said he would be sending me one of the good colts the following spring to use in the park. It was quite common for the ranch hands to try and match up the outgoing colts with wardens they thought would be a good fit. This was indeed an endorsement. The following spring, I worked diligently with the filly and was even able to ride her in the Calgary Stampede Parade.

Ranch life settled down to a normal routine under Cal Hayes's direction, but by 1971 the future of the ranch was once again under scrutiny. The elk numbers had never really decreased, despite harvesting of varying intensity over the years. The first year Hayes became foreman, in 1969, the province declared a special hunting season and 53 elk were shot. This put little dent in a herd approaching 1,500 elk. In 1970, hunting was stepped up to issuing 70 permits a week for a total of six weeks. This was never a pleasant time for the staff working at the ranch, as there seemed no end to the constant bang of rifles, the increased road traffic, partying and loud noise emanating from the campground. They constantly worried some hunter would shoot a horse. Though it was prudent to wear a red vest, they never felt quite safe going out for a ride.

In 1971, the Alberta Fish and Game Association stepped up its pressure to have

Hunters passing through the Ya Ha Tinda.

the horses removed from the ranch in favour of elk. The association wrote a letter to Don Mazankowski, the federal MP representing the riding, complaining about grass consumption by the horses. This was resolutely rebutted by Director J.I. "Black" Jack Nicol, considered to be one of the last firm leaders in the parks service. Nicol put a lid on the issue while he was in office, but it did not put the matter completely to rest.[119]

One new development not to Cal Hayes's liking was having to submit monthly reports to the regional office. The regional office was gradually extending its power, like any other bureaucratic organization, over all aspects of park administration. By the mid-1970s, Banff had little say over the daily fate of the Ya Ha Tinda and Hayes's reports went directly to Calgary. The regional office must have developed some serious clout, as former Chief Park Warden Mitchell was now national park supervisor for the region and still wanted to get rid of the ranch. He still saw it

as a game sanctuary that was being threatened by overgrazing from horses. He had a valid concern. As the 1980s progressed, the pressure from both horses and elk began seriously impacting the once lush rough fescue grasslands. Shrubby cinquefoil and dense thickets of dwarf (bog) birch became more common.[120] This was likely due to the fire control policies of the time, and the grazing off of grass cover that once carried the frequent burns lit by Aboriginal people to attract bison, elk and bighorn sheep.[121] Not only were shrubs increasing but forest cover also expanded. The hills that had been open bare slopes in the early 1900s were now flush with stands of thick lodgepole pine and groves of trembling aspen. The cool, north-facing slopes were gradually filling with native white spruce. The wetter ground spawned willow growth that soon invaded the grassy meadows, reducing forage as competition for soil increased. The open montane of early years was gradually becoming crowded out, a process that continues to this day.

Bert Pittaway, the chief park warden in Banff, was determined to keep the ranch, despite the growing concern over loss of elk habitat. He actually had an ally in Jim Sime in the Western Regional Office, who had a strong warden background and did not want to see the horse program lost to the warden service. The hunting pressure had not significantly dented the population, so they decided to try trapping and relocating the elk. Though they had some small success, anyone who has tried to herd elk into a corral knows how difficult this is. Unlike horses, they just scatter to the wind, often charging straight back at the riders. It required too much manpower with too little success and was soon abandoned.

In frustration, discussions got underway in 1985 between Parks Canada and Alberta's fish and wildlife division to actively manage the range to see if sufficient improvements could be made to support both horse and elk populations. This resulted in the interdepartmental Ya Ha Tinda Ranch Elk Management Committee.[122]

Though Cal Hayes probably saw the benefits of range improvement, he probably had a few good words to say about having to sit on this committee as ranch foreman. His input would be required, as he knew the movements of both the horses and elk and the best place for extending hay production. While Hayes took on more of the administrative duties of the ranch, helped considerably by Moe Vroom, who was much more acquainted with reports and bookkeeping, the daily chores and training did not stop.

As mentioned earlier, Slim Haugen, who started working at the ranch with Fred Dixon, later became ranch foreman. He was a classic cowboy who hailed from North Dakota but moved to Canada as a young man. He was tall, quiet and excellent with horses. In his younger years, he gained much of his experience working on the larger spreads in British Columbia, such as the Eldorado Ranch near Kelowna and the famous Douglas Lake Ranch near Merritt. Most of his time on these big spreads was spent breaking and training wild horses. Haugen worked for the government first as a farrier and barn boss in Yoho National Park before moving on to the Ya Ha Tinda. While working in Yoho, Jim Sime was the chief park warden. On one auspicious occasion, around the mid-1950s, Haugen was instrumental in helping Sime find and rescue a young girl stranded on Mount Field, for which Sime received a commendation from federal Cabinet Minister Jean Lesage. They climbed up through the night before finding her trapped on a 12-inch ledge overlooking a 600-foot drop. Haugen was able to lower Sime to the woman, who then brought her up to higher ground. It was a cold and rainy night, making it miserable for all of them. It was dawn before a public safety team could reach them and get them all safely off the mountain. No one doubted she would not have survived the

Gord Patterson
saddling a horse
in the barn.

COURTESY KATHY
PATTERSON COLLECTION.

night if they had not found her. Haugen was no climber, but he was capable on tough ground and always kept his head.[123]

Haugen became foreman of the Ya Ha Tinda in 1974, taking over from Bill Burles, who held the foreman position since 1968. (Burles had worked for Don Sutherland, and when Sutherland resigned, Burles took the position.) Haugen loved the time he spent on the Ya Ha Tinda and held the position until he retired in 1982. His retirement party must

have been aided by his favourite drink, white rum and honey. During Haugen's tenure, the ranch employed more than the usual number of ranch hands, possibly due to the many new work projects and research now being undertaken. The month-end reports would still be part of the job, as would some of the administrative aspects of attending meetings. In all likelihood, Haugen was as computer illiterate as Cal Hayes, which may be why the number of employees doubled the following year. The year

1975 saw a large turnover of staff, most of who stayed for only short periods of time. At one point, there were no fewer than nine employees living on the ranch. One of them was Gord Patterson, who started working there in 1971. The once quiet ranch was teeming with people, which mitigated but did not eliminate the isolation.

Patterson was working as a cowboy for Paul Peyto in Lake Louise when he had the chance to get a full-time job at the Ya Ha Tinda in 1974 after he married his wife Kathy. Another ranch hand working there was Buddy Hamilton, a good friend of the Pattersons. Hamilton was thinking of leaving the ranch for other work in the near future, which would leave Haugen short-handed. To avoid this, Haugen asked Hamilton if Patterson would take his old job back as a permanent employee. Patterson had loved the ranch from the first time he saw it and was more than pleased to return. His wife Kathy had visited the Ya Ha Tinda when Patterson first worked there and though she had some apprehension about the isolation, she felt it was a good move for them. By now, they had a small family with a daughter, Leah, born the year before. She was also pregnant with her second daughter, Wendy.

The five years the Pattersons spent there were some of the best years of Kathy's life. By then, the Western Regional Office had taken over all aspects of running the ranch, but this suited Kathy fine, as the person in charge was Jim Sime. If anyone embodied the life and soul of a park warden, it was Sime. He had started out as a seasonal park warden and rose steadily to chief park warden, and then moved on to the regional office. He was far-sighted and fair-minded and knew when to let people do the job they were hired for. He was also Kathy's boss a few years later, when she was hired to look after the Bighorn Campground. If she needed anything, she just asked Sime. Kathy remembers particularly that Jim Sime always insisted they consider the place home.

Gord Patterson was also happy to be working for Slim Haugen, who was easygoing and a good hand with horses. It had made a difference in the decision to return, as his relationship with Cal Hayes, who was foreman in 1971, was not always amicable. Patterson considered Hayes "old school" when it came to breaking and training horses, though he did have a good reputation for handling stallions. Patterson had a gentle hand with horses and animals in general and was patient and observant in his training methods. Kathy always thought of him as having skills akin to the "horse whisperer" – a story based on Buck Brannaman's life as a horse trainer.

Though Haugen was brought up break-ing and training horses in the rough manner typical of the early West, he was gentle with all animals himself and had no problem with Patterson's willingness to work patiently with young colts. There was a mutual respect and friendship that created an almost extended family atmosphere, with the addition of Kathy and the children's presence.

When the Pattersons arrived in 1974, the staff was still considerable – indeed, In 1975 the staff was up to nine people, which included Cal Sime, who helped Kathy look after the campground, among other duties. It was also about then that Luigi Morgantini from the University of Alberta began his research on the elk movement at the ranch. This was the beginning of extensive research on the elk at the ranch through the univer-sity that would eventually include researchers from the University of Montana. Morgantini was welcomed at the ranch, though the ranch

hands would often try and get the better of him. Kathy remembers her husband stealing Morgantini's max/min thermometer and putting it in the oven. When Morgantini shook them down to reveal the true temperature, some of the jokes lost their punch. They could never fool him at crib either, as he had a keen and observant eye as to how the game was played and did not lose often.[124]

What Kathy particularly remembers, however, was her husband taking great care to select a quiet horse for Morgantini to ride to aid in following the elk. As his skill grew and the elk went farther afield, Morgantini was also given a pack horse and taught to pack. Kathy was amazed. She always felt sorry for the young man with the strong Italian accent heading out on his lonely excursions to camp with the elk, for more days than she can remember – in winter, summer, spring or fall. These excursions alone, deep into the prairies of the Ya Ha Tinda, left a lasting attachment for the ranch with Morgantini. Much later, when other government agencies tried to gain control of the ranch, he was vociferous in defending it as a unique habitat for wildlife. In fact, Morgantini was so effective that Gaby Fortin, future chief park warden of Banff and ultimately director general in the regional office, would comment, "No one really knew of the Ya Ha Tinda in government until Luigi brought it to their attention."[125]

The Pattersons spent six years on the ranch, all of which were quiet in terms of political interference. It was also a time of plenty. Kathy remembers that at the end of each fiscal year money budgeted for the ranch was often left over. They dared not lose it, so Haugen and Patterson would almost have a spending spree, buying new saddles and other equipment that needed replacing. During their stay, Kathy had her second child Wendy and, with many friends and relations living close by, they never missed a chance to enjoy family events. Halloween was a must and no one's birthday

went uncelebrated. Christmas was just as special for them as any family, or maybe more so given the special place they lived. Gord Patterson would go out every Christmas on his horse and find just the right sized tree, which would be skidded back for decoration. The Christmas season always helped ease the staff into the winter ahead, especially January, when most of the daily activity slowed to a crawl. Winter cold and blowing winds pinned everyone down but the hunters. During their stay, the elk population was still soaring and they accumulated in large numbers on their winter range. The government allowed a winter draw for elk in January to cull as many as it could. No one left the house or went for a ride until the hunt was over. The hunters that came in were often inexperienced, and the danger of getting shot was very real. Somehow, the hunters managed to distinguish the elk from the horses, however, as there was never any reported concern about losing too many horses from hunting activity. The only one who ventured out was the intrepid Morgantini, who felt he still had to keep track of the elk movement, particularly with the hunting pressure.

In many ways, the Patterson children were brought up much like any farm kid on the prairies before the turn of the century, with the exception that they had all the modern

Gord Patterson driving the buggy in the yard.

COURTESY KATHY PATTERSON COLLECTION.

conveniences of running water, electricity and a phone line. The girls were used to the horses, which became surrogate playmates. Patterson even managed to find a small wagon that he hitched to a pony to pull the girls around in – although he probably had the most fun with it. The girls became so used to the horses, they thought nothing of going out with Haugen when he turned the colts out to pasture. On one occasion, a young colt trotted by Patterson's daughter Leah, who reached out to pet it. The startled colt jumped and landed a light kick on her leg. With great seriousness, Leah turned to

Haugen and warned him, "You better be careful, because the horses might kick you!"[126]

Like all families with young children on the ranch, the day came when home-schooling was not practical and the budding interest of their children required daily interaction with others their own age. They needed to go to school and meet the world that would start the long journey to adulthood. The day before they left the ranch in 1979, Gord and Kathy Patterson rode alone to Eagle Lake, where they could see all of the Ya Ha Tinda spread out to the west. Kathy suddenly realized how hard it would be to leave, as there could never be another home quite like it.

Brian King was one employee who stayed at the ranch for two years with his family. He actually arrived just before Slim Haugen retired. After Haugen retired in 1982, Cal Hayes returned yet again to be foreman of the Ya Ha Tinda but stayed this time until he retired from the government. The King family enjoyed the two years they stayed there and enjoyed Hayes's company. King considered Hayes to be the best man he had ever worked for with regard to moving or trailing horses. He mentions that Hayes picked up this skill when he gathered horses with his brothers as youth near Hanna. "He told me that he and his brothers used to gather bunches of horses that farmers had turned loose after replacing them with tractors." The Hayes brothers would trail the captured horses to Red Top Packers in Calgary, on the north side of the river and west of where the current Calgary Zoo is located. Brian recalls, "I had a fellow tell me later that the Hayes boys couldn't read brands too well."[127]

One of the more interesting developments that happened when King was working there was a change in how they returned the horses to the four mountain parks of Banff, Yoho, Kootenay and Glacier. In 1984, Gaby Fortin from Parks Canada's Quebec region took a term assignment as chief park warden in Banff. He immediately became a great horse enthusiast. He also envied the days when horses were trailed back to the various parks via Banff and decided to reinstate the practice. He felt it was a great opportunity to get to know his staff while having a bit of an "old boys" get-together. Accordingly, he invited those wardens who had sufficient experience to handle the ride and not be a liability. Anyone invited was thrilled and could not help but feel a certain amount of pride that they were considered. It soon became a privilege to be invited on the drive. One thing Fortin was fair about was to make sure there was a representative for the horses from each park, as they knew their own animals.

This ride, traditionally a well-planned men's bonding party, hit a glitch one year. My husband, Dale Portman, the warden dog handler from Lake Louise, with a lifetime of experience with horses, was sufficiently up the ladder to be asked along. The fact that he had considerable experience chasing horses made him an excellent choice for the drive. He happily returned home to tell me the good news. I had never seen him so excited. He never really thought about the fact that I was also a warden with fairly decent riding ability. Nevertheless, I happily reported Dale going on the trip to Earl Hayes, now the Yoho barn boss and the first choice to go as the Yoho representative. To my surprise, just a day before the big event, Hayes announced he could not go because of a family event. It was early in the season and no one else with horse experience was at work. I brought the matter up with the Chief Park Warden Gordon Rutherford and it was decided I would be the most experienced person to go in lieu of Hayes. Not believing my good fortune, and completely ignorant of the significance of the event as a male-bonding getaway, I told Dale that evening that I was going too.

My exhilaration at going on this great adventure with my husband was met with stunned horror. Not only was a woman suddenly going – it happened to be his wife. Dale's mortification knew no bounds. He threatened divorce. He pleaded for me to reconsider. He refused to talk to me and said I could find my own way there. He would certainly not drive me to his ultimate humiliation. When I found a ride with his "turncoat" neighbour, park warden Dale Loewen, he convinced himself that Gaby Fortin would immediately send me home. At best he thought I would lose my nerve and opt out once the chips were down. He took the wrong approach by muttering about how hard it was to chase horses and that I would make a fool of myself.

Finally, the morning of departure arrived and two warden trucks headed out of Lake Louise.

Dale was fuming in his own truck as he followed the other two driving ahead, obviously chatting amiably. He was still muttering furiously to himself about his turncoat neighbour when they turned into the Banff horse corrals just before dawn. To his surprise, not one of the ten wardens invited along said a word when I jumped out of Loewen's truck. No luck there. Nothing was mentioned as we proceeded to the Ya Ha Tinda where Banff barn boss, Johnny Nylund, had organized everything. Each person was given a choice of the horse they wanted for the drive from their own park horses. They used these horses year after year and it was presumed they would know which horse would have the best speed, control and bottom for the chase ahead. I was not surprised when Dale picked one of the best of the Yoho horses, as he had worked there for some time and knew Flirt to be a great horse for the chase. Theoretically, I could have upped him on this, but Flirt would not have been my first choice anyway. I chose instead a fast, very sound little quarter horse named Charcoal, whom I had ridden a lot. When the ranch hands tried to catch him, however, he was still winter fresh and they had to lasso him when they could not corner him on foot. They looked at me, puzzled, and asked, "Are you sure you want him?" All the men watched as I saddled the black gelding, watching every move the jittery horse made. I knew at that point the best thing to do was take him for a long walk and mount in some quiet place. I rode placidly back to the crowd just as the chase was about to begin.

By then, everyone was focused on the task ahead with every man (and woman!) for themselves and devil take the hindmost. With a thunder, 150 head of horses were turned loose with two riders heading for the trail to Scotch Camp at a dead run. The first 15 kilometres were some of the wildest riding most of them had ever done. There was no chance to assess the terrain ahead – it was enough just to keep up. At one point, Dale happened to see me and another warden out flanking a bunch trying to pull away and he had never seen anyone happier. The next two days still required some crazy riding through the timber or open flats, until the herd finally started to settle down.

Dale finally came to terms with me being part of the crew when no one else seemed to object. In fact, I fit in and had no interest in seeking his company – I had plenty of other people to talk to. I mentioned to Dale some time later that Gaby Fortin's only comment on my unexpected participation was, "Sure a good thing you can ride."

Neil Plested, who brought his family with him, replaced Brian King in 1985. Management was becoming more and more open to having the men there with their wives and children, though it often meant they did not stay long after the kids reached school age. Some families opted for home-schooling for a year or more but often moved on when the kids got older and needed interaction with children their own age. When the Plesteds moved there, their youngest daughter was only a few months old, but they stayed for five years anyway. In total, there were four Plested children, each with a special memory of growing up in this unique environment. It is interesting to hear their stories from such a young perspective, free of adult problems or political developments. They just saw the world immediately in front of them. When they were old enough to ride, they were given a Shetland pony. Oak Plested, who was three when they moved there, says she remembers "riding my horse Buddy who was a half quarter horse, half Shetland pony. In the summer I would often ride with my father and Cal Hayes down to the Bighorn Falls, the campground and many other places in the mountains."[128] They had the ubiquitous dog and often went fishing in Scalp Creek. During the winter, they played hockey when not being home-schooled. The big night of the week was going to Hayes's house to watch *Hockey Night in Canada*.

Kathy Calvert riding in gymkhana.

One event almost ended their happy story tale. Oak's sister Dawn recalls,

One vivid memory I have is of the time my sister, Brook, fell over the cliff by Scalp Creek. We were playing on the top above the creek and I had the idea to 'tidy up' the plateau. I suggested we pick up the branches and rocks that were littered about the bank and toss them over the edge. We were all busily engaged with this task when I looked around for Brook. She was nowhere to be found. After a quick, frantic search, we discovered she had fallen over the side and had landed on a small ledge about four feet below the edge. I dispatched Oak in search of our parents and I climbed down to where Brook had fallen. I had Leaf lay down and while I tried to boost her, I had Leaf try to pull her up. I remember thinking she had gotten really heavy when she suddenly lightened and was pulled up. My Dad pulled me up next and that was the last time for several months that we were allowed to play in this area.

Dawn Plested recalls her time there as being "something out of a story book. I had the opportunity to grow a very close relationship with my siblings and most of my memories include playing and exploring with my brother and sisters."[129]

Despite the periods of calm and growth for the Ya Ha Tinda as a horse ranch for the warden service, this role was again challenged in the mid-1980s. The driving force behind eliminating the horse presence continued to be the growing elk numbers and the depletion of the range. The efforts at range improvement that resulted in clearing an extra 93 hectares of land by 1985 seemed only to exacerbate the problems, which ultimately led to what historian Jim Taylor referred to as "Range Wars."[130] Another intergovernmental committee was formed called the Ya Ha Tinda Ranch Elk Management Committee. Its immediate task was to deal with the emergence of well-defined interest groups who allied with the long-standing interests of the provincial government's agencies. This was a serious threat to the continued existence of the Ya Ha Tinda as a government horse ranch independent of the province.

The premise that the Ya Ha Tinda could be both an important wildlife habitat and a horse ranch was recognized as a complex management problem, often aggravated by confused leadership at the regional level, which was staggering under federal demands for cost-cutting programs. (Proper management of ranch land can provide good habitat for both horses and wildlife, which is certainly preferable to using the land for golf courses or campgrounds).

Photo by: J. Marie Nylund

The bountiful money of the early 1980s was beginning to dry up. Suddenly, the ranch was faced with "new ways of doing business." It was largely due to the "grit and determination of the warden service to hang on to what had almost become a sacred trust."[131] The ranch not only provided the wardens with horses that supported a way of life that was impossible without them but it was almost mythically seen as the heritage and heart of the warden service. The wardens were not going to lose it without a fight.

Though the added range addition helped somewhat, the elk born on the ranch were less prone to migrate beyond its borders, where hunters of every variety awaited. Natural predators were always present, but human encroachment and increased hunting contributed to the elk remaining on the ranch, particularly in spring when they would normally migrate to the high country. With young calves in tow, this exodus was not so enticing.

Despite the high numbers of elk on the ranch and the eastern slopes of the mountains, the horses continued to be seen as a threat to the elk herd. Pressure increased from the range management committee to remove the horses altogether. The proposed solution was to move the ranching operation to another location. Again, a land swap was proposed. Various areas were suggested, such as land nearer to Sundre, where the ranch hands would be free of the problem wildlife. The administrators in the regional office in Calgary had changed dramatically over the years and directors rarely had a connection to the warden service. They had no real understanding of the horses, their function within the organization or the place the Ya Ha Tinda held in the hearts of the warden service. A land swap was seriously considered with the province and almost accepted. This proposal could not be kept quiet, however, and counter-arguments came vociferously to the forefront. The best and most cogent defense of keeping the ranch came from Yoho Chief Park Warden Gordon Rutherford, who wrote,

The ranch and horse use is important to the warden service. The horse is considered the most effective and most appropriate way to do many aspects of the warden job and a good horse breeding, training and winter program is necessary to supply the "tools" of that job. The Ya Ha Tinda has supplied those tools and at the same time has supplied the tradition and mindset needed to allow a predominantly urban and academically trained warden service to be able to use and care for horses in a backcountry situation.[132]

Ironically, it was concern for the elk that ultimately saved the ranch. The province, with the aggressive development within Kananaskis Country and Peter Lougheed Provincial Park, had lost a great deal of creditability with environmentalists as good stewards of the land. They tended to view the provincial government as a bit rapacious when it came to exploiting its own natural resources. There was more conviction that the federal government would actually do a better job of protecting the elk and the habitat. A vigorous writing campaign on the part of the public and nongovernmental environmental groups finally persuaded the federal government to drop the issue and keep the ranch. The development of large golf courses and a ski area on the boundary of their premier provincial park was just a bit too ill-considered for most people to take the provincial government seriously as a steward for the environment.

However, there were reassuring signs. The Alberta government began to restrict motor vehicle access to public lands in the provincial portions of the upper Clearwater, Red Deer and Panther watersheds, and officials recognized that the Bighorn Wildland surrounding the Ya Ha Tinda had exceptional recreational and ecological value.

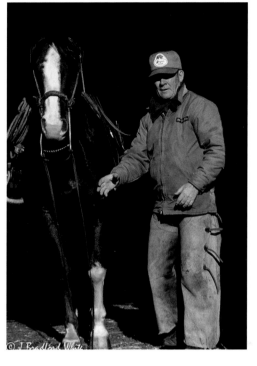

Clockwise from top right:

Foreman Cal Hayes going for a ride.

PHOTO BY BRADFORD WHITE.

Bighorn Back-country Map.

Christmas tree hunting with the Pigeon children.

PHOTO BY KEN PIGEON.

Wrangler Dick Levie leaving the barn in early morning.

PHOTO BY BRADFORD WHITE.

117

CHAPTER 5
RESOLUTION TO AN ELUSIVE FUTURE

The Ya Ha Tinda ranch plays a key role for the entire Banff National Park Central Rockies ecosystem. It really is the hub of a wheel for the entire park ecosystem.
—Mark Hebblewhite

The 1990s began auspiciously at the ranch, when it seemed the status of the Ya Ha Tinda was resolved and no longer a bother to the upper management. Regional office administrators agreed that horse use was integral to the warden service and, for the present, the Ya Ha Tinda seemed the best place to fulfill this need. But this did not last long. The prevailing wind whispered that maintaining the ranch could only be accomplished with cost-cutting measures. The 1980s had almost been excessive, with federal money being handed out, often spent freely on trivial things just to use up the allotted budget. One mountain rescue warden recalls a climbing trip to Kluane National Park where he was offered a helicopter ride to see the vast park just to use up the substantial amount of money designated for fighting fires. The

motto for everything back then was "use it or lose it."[133]

That changed dramatically by the early to mid-1990s, when the money began to dry up. After decades of fiscal deficits under both Liberal and Progressive Conservative governments, the Liberals finally tried to reverse the trend. The re-evaluation of spending money on the ranch came out of a larger financial policy implemented by the Liberal government to reduce Canada's soaring deficit. In 1994, then federal Minister of Finance Paul Martin imposed a spending freeze, forcing all departments to look for ways to save money. Parks Canada was at that time administered by the Department of the Environment but was soon to be transferred to the Department of Heritage and Culture, where it would have a much

Mark Hebblewhite glassing for collared elk.

smaller profile. Under that department, all revenue was put into a big pot and redistributed according to need. Parks Canada was small and did not have much of a squeaky wheel. Most of the revenue it generated went into the pot but very little came back. To solve this problem, it was proposed that Parks Canada become an agency (essentially, a business) so that money generated by parks would stay with parks.[134]

The spending freeze imposed an austerity program on the ranch budget, and soon the regional office was looking for more efficient ways of raising horses. Business principles were adopted and each operational unit had to come up with a business plan. An independent consultant was hired to assess the ranch operation, which, yet again, nearly spelled the end of the Ya Ha Tinda as a government horse ranch. The consultant's report, with no apparent collaboration, concluded it was too costly to grow hay to feed the horses the ranch had. He recommended the ranching operation be moved to the Bar U Ranch National Historic Site south of Longview, Alberta.[135]

In 1991, Parks Canada acquired the Bar U Ranch to commemorate Canada's ranching heritage. It has 148 hectares (367 acres) of land, including the ranch's headquarters area. To many in the regional office it seemed the most appropriate place to raise the park horses, as it is situated in the middle of Alberta's ranching country. Chief Park Warden Perry Jacobson, then acting superintendent in Kootenay National Park, recalls, "Mike Schintz was tasked with finding an alternate for the Ya Ha Tinda – I think this was a Regional project looking at cost savings. The Bar U was considered but abandoned for lack of space (The Bar U is just over a half-section in size). There was even a ridiculous suggestion of finding grazing leases out East of the Bar U."[136]

The Rocky Mountain Elk Foundation was all for this. In 1994, it submitted a proposal to Parks Canada that it take over the management of the Ya Ha Tinda and have it run jointly between the foundation and parks. With this arrangement, the foundation, with help from Parks Canada, could manage the Ya Ha Tinda strictly for the protection of the elk. With the high population found there at that time, one wonders what the elk needed protection from. A more cynical view led many to suspect it was just a cover to have an unlimited supply of elk for big game hunters under the "management" guise of the foundation. Nevertheless, this new co-management approach was quickly becoming the way of the future and seemed to satisfy the business-plan approach to running the national parks (also considered de rigueur for any success). Jacobson, who was the chief park warden of the Kootenay-Yoho-Lake Louise Field Unit, and had the responsibility of the ranch at the time, reflects, "We damn near lost the ranch at that point."[137]

But the proposal from the elk foundation even had some managers in Parks Canada blinking – it was just too species-oriented for everyone to swallow. In response, the wardens prepared their own financial report, detailing ways of making the ranch more cost-effective and consistent with ecological and historical values. They presented an alternative plan to reduce costs by implementing more strategic grazing strategies and cutting capital costs. Fortunately, most of the essential buildings needed to operate the ranch had been built during the flush years. They also presented a strong argument against the Rocky Mountain Elk Foundation's use of the land. Quite rightly they pointed out it went against all sound environmental principles to protect the land for just one species. This simplistic plan held no place for predators, which were necessary to keep the elk and other game healthy. The bookkeepers in the regional office could find no calculations to refute these arguments and, once again, the ranch seemed to achieve a measure of stability when the foundation's offer was rejected. Jacobson adds, "Anyway, the quest fell through the cracks."[138]

A spot of good luck finally put an end to moving the ranch to the Bar U or any other distant pasture in Alberta. In July 1996, Ms. Suzan Hurtubise, the assistant deputy minister of the environment, visited the western region with the mandate to establish the change in government policy to make Parks Canada an agency. At that point, the ranch was managed by Darro Stinson, the superintendent of the new management unit nicknamed KYLL (an acronym for Kootenay, Yoho and Lake Louise) who reported to Donna Petrachenko in the Western Regional Office. Knowing the Ya Ha Tinda was on the cutting block, Stinson, a devout supporter of the ranch, asked Hurtubise if she would care to take a look at the ranch. She agreed and soon Darro, Petrachenko and Hurtubise were flying over the soaring mountains that sheltered the beautiful prairie grasslands. It is rumoured that the vision of free-ranging horses on the prairies at the foot of the Rockies, and the sight of the well-established, functional buildings, prompted her to exclaim, "What do you want to sell this for? It is beautiful!"[139] Her reaction seems to have dampened the problem of the ranch, which was, once again, put on low simmer.

This was not a pleasant time for the ranch's foreman, Cal Hayes. He was a man coming close to retirement and the new management requirements were not part of his heritage. He was a horseman and wrangler who knew how to deal with running a ranch that did not require spending most of his day sweating over budget reports, time sheets and management meetings. He was happy to see that the ranch was not lost, but by 1993 he was ready for retirement. But when he went, it was with a good conscience, knowing the management would be taken over by capable younger men. Hayes had spent many years at the ranch and had witnessed the evolution of its function through the numerous changes in administration. He had been a firm and popular foreman, and his retirement was one of the biggest parties the ranch had ever seen. Even now, his spirit remains there, guiding a new generation of stewards tasked with upholding the long, time-honoured vision of the true purpose of the ranch.

Ken Pigeon and his wife Debbie were the first of this next generation to pick up the challenge. They moved to the ranch in 1988, with a solid background working with horses and outfitters. Debbie Pigeon also had several years of experience working as a backcountry cook for her father, Clint Coleman, and his outfitting business in Jasper. Ken Pigeon was happy to get the job offer at the Ya Ha Tinda after a few nomadic years with his wife, working for different outfits in the mountains that offered only summer work. The biggest advantage for Pigeon, when he started in 1988, was a chance to work with Cal Hayes. This made it much easier to assume the mantle of foreman, by learning the essentials from a man who had spent most of his life doing the job. But Pigeon also realized Hayes was from an older generation and things were changing fast in the world they worked in. Some of Hayes's methods were set in stone and did not necessarily apply to the people the ranch had to supply horses to.

When the Pigeons moved to the ranch, they did not have any children. Not long after moving to the ranch, their son Clinton was born, followed by their daughter Jessie a few years later. This was actually a delight for Hayes, who "was awesome with families. He liked little kids and old dogs." Pigeon recalls that Hayes was "not the best horseman but he had an interesting way with horses – especially studs."[140] Hayes would not tolerate a cantankerous horse and worked particularly hard with studs that could be unpredictable.

When Pigeon first worked at the ranch as a ranch hand in 1988, the elk herd was close to its apex. An aerial survey conducted by Alberta Fish and Wildlife throughout the eastern slopes came up with 2,700 head of elk. At any one time, the riders on the ranch could encounter

Debbie and Ken Pigeon with kids on horseback.

up to 800 head on a single day. Because of the range problem, the men were kept busy in a daily chase to keep the elk off the hay needed for the horses. Pigeon smiles as he describes the difficultly doing this:

You'd go feed first thing in the morning and by 2 pm the elk would start moving in and chasing the horses off the hay. So we got this brilliant idea that if the elk were going to chase our horses off the hay ... then we would chase them off. Have you ever tried to chase 800 head of elk? You don't chase them ... they scatter! It's just horrible! I remember one time, they went right through the fence in the Little Bighorn Field ... and went across that road that went to the Clearwater ... just as these natives were driving up. All these elk ran across,

going wide open in front of their truck. They stopped us and said, "You guys seen any elk?" I said, "Yes, but I don't think you want any of them; they are a little hot!" When you get 800 head of elk in front of you and – when they start doing the snake – a snake like movement of the head and neck – and they are about five abreast. It makes it very interesting.[141]

Though the elk culling continued through hunting activity, an elk relocation program was also begun. This latter program had limited success. Relocating the elk was not successful if older cows were caught, as they were conditioned to the ranch and soon returned unless they were killed or fenced in. Relocating younger cow elk was moderately more successful. But the hunting remained a problem for all those living on the ranch. Hunters would come from all across Alberta, but often Aboriginal hunters showed up just a week before Christmas, as if they were looking for turkeys rather than elk. Many of these hunters were not very selective. The Pigeons recalled, "But they'd shoot … just herd shoot [into the herd] … it was just like a war going on out there. And they get all these elk … and they had this little tiny team (of horses) and this wagon to haul the elk. We were out feeding (one day) and they came over to us and asked, 'Would you mind hauling some elk out for us?' Cal just looked at them and said, 'If you'd get some of those God damned (yahoos) off the wagon you could haul your own elk!' They just turned around and drove away."[142]

On one occasion, warden Mac Elder had just brought a load of horses back to the ranch for the winter when he agreed to help Hayes feed some of the mares in the pasture below the house. They set out with the empty hay wagon for the large stack of loose hay kept near the Quonset hut, intending to stack a load for distribution to the horses in the field below. Elder recalls, "We were just getting near that pile of hay when all hell broke loose! All we could do was hide behind that stack until the hunters finished shooting the hell out of the place."[143] To Elder's disbelief, neither one of them had

been shot, and it appeared all the horses were still standing. A lot of hunting was done from the Cascade Fire Road leading to the ranch from the Banff National Park boundary. By 1985, when this was finally closed to the public, much of the hunting problems stopped.

After Ken Pigeon became foreman, he felt free to address a slowly simmering problem with a new generation of young wardens. When, in the early 1900s, Chief Warden Howard Sibbald first started hiring men for this job, they came from farming, ranching or an outfitting business and had, with little exception, good experience with horses and backcountry skills. Their education was usually minimal, but the service was not looking for men with university degrees. They needed people with practical outdoor skills. After the Second World War, many of the men hired on were war vets who knew horses and had solid survival skills. They were strong, independent, often solitary men who relished the isolation of the backcountry. But major changes occurred in the mid-1960s with a report by Jim Sime and Don Schuler, altering the face of the warden service. The report acknowledged that the national parks needed visitors to survive, but most of those people were staying mainly in the front country or townsites, having little desire for a backcountry experience. The pattern of use and type of people coming to the park was changing rapidly and the administration responded. It decided to centralize the warden service to one reporting office in each park. The practice of maintaining a district year-round was abandoned, and backcountry wardens were forced to move to town during the winter. The typical park visitor was also more cosmopolitan, and it was felt the new wardens coming on should have more education.[144]

Mountain rescue was suddenly a big addition to the many hats wardens wore, as rash young adventurers tackled the mountains, invariably getting hurt, stranded or killed. The older wardens were not impressed with this new challenge, seeing the end of a way of life they had loved. Though the pool of young applicants for the warden service was growing, fewer and fewer came from a farm or ranching background. This began to have an impact on the principal job of the ranch hand at the Ya Ha Tinda, tasked with turning out reliable horses for the new recruits. Suddenly, ranch staff found they were giving colts that needed more "rounding out" to young, fresh-faced wardens who knew little about horses. The staff would nervously watch these wardens ride off in the spring with their saddle horse and two pack horses, which they probably just learned to pack the day before they left, crossing their fingers and hoping they would at least get off the ranch before having a wreck.

Ultimately, the inevitable happened in 1979. Neil Colgan was a typical, keen, young warden assigned to the Red Deer River District for the summer who had minimal horse experience. The details of his death are not known, other than he had tied his horses up while checking out Douglas Lake campground when one of the horses kicked him, rupturing his spleen. At some point he realized he was dying but managed to write a short farewell note to his parents and build a small fire, which he lay beside. He lay his arms across his chest and died. His horses were eventually found back at the Sandhills warden cabin on the Red Deer River after he failed to respond to the scheduled radio call. Colgan is buried in Mountain View Cemetery in Banff.[145]

Chief Park Warden Perry Jacobson had seen many young wardens go out by themselves with little more experience than Colgan and was amazed that serious accidents or death did not happen more frequently. He knew there were many close calls that could have been serious, but no major injury has been recorded in the backcountry since Colgan's death.

Still, it was a wake-up call for Banff, which now insisted that if one radio call was missed, help would be on the way – usually by helicopter. Banff also decided that, whenever possible, wardens in the backcountry should travel in pairs. The much bigger Jasper National Park did not adopt these policies and wardens continued to travel alone for many years thereafter. (No one got too excited in Jasper unless the warden had not been heard from after three missed radio calls). It also forced the Ya Ha Tinda staff to take a harder look at a warden's experience with horses and whether the horses they were getting were trained sufficiently to be safe for staff that knew little about the animal.[146]

In 1968, the Ya Ha Tinda was gifted with an RCMP thoroughbred stallion called Brun, along with nine brood mares and five foals, when Fort Walsh in Cypress Hills was closed down. The ranch eventually received 68 horses from the RCMP over the years. The thoroughbred brood mares from the RCMP were high-strung and though they threw good colts with intelligence and stamina, they could be hard to handle. These large black horses soon gained a reputation for being "hot" and were given to those wardens with the most experience. But a quieter, easier to handle horse was needed and management started leaning to other breeds of horse to mingle with the existing stock. With direction from the regional office, the ranch staff began buying quieter quarter horses and

even wound up with a Morgan stallion that gave very good colts.

During the years that Ken Pigeon worked at the Ya Ha Tinda, he worked with a number of different ranch hands. Steve Bennett, an easy-going man and good with colts, worked with Hayes and Pigeon for four years, and they missed him when he left. Todd McCready, already well known as an outstanding mountain rescue helicopter pilot, switched careers and worked at the ranch for a few years. Tom McCready, Todd's father, was one of the best outfitters in Jasper, so Todd grew up knowing horses. An unfortunate accident with a colt broke his pelvis and he returned to Jasper. He was another hand they were sad to see go. For both Hayes and Pigeon, it brought home how dangerous the job could be, even for experienced horse handlers. On one occasion, they noticed Bennett down in the far pasture, riding around in circles. The scene looked so odd, Hayes said, "You've got to get that Bennett. He's goofy in the head." It turned out Bennett had been bucked off and had hit his head hard on the ground. He was soon packed off to the hospital, where he was treated for a concussion.[147] The ranch hands were always amazed each fall when the new wardens returned with their horses and themselves intact. The wardens had just spent the summer alone in the bush, often

Ken Pigeon and Cal Hayes at Hayes's retirement party.

COURTESY KEN AND DEBBIE PIGEON COLLECTION.

learning by trial and error how to keep themselves and their horses safe and work-ready. Most rewarding, perhaps, was the crazy grin the new recruits sported when they showed up in one piece after facing the challenges of the trail, the horses, the work and their own loneliness.

In 1994, Ken Pigeon found he had inherited a system and a way of life on the ranch that was well tested, and he saw no reason to make drastic changes. He was, however, free to implement some programs he had always wanted to see. The new recruits had a lot to learn about horses and could not be relied upon to deal with unseasoned colts in the field. Pigeon decided that not only should the colts have an extra year of training but it would be smart to give the wardens some training as well. He soon had permission to hold a week-long horse school for the untrained staff. Marie Nylund, secretary/treasurer of the Park Warden Service Alumni Society and former employee at the Ya Ha Tinda from 1997 to 2003, summed up how she understood the training course came about:

> Prior to us going to the ranch Ken had consulted with (park warden) Dale Loewen and other wardens about how the course would be taught and they wrote up a horsemanship manual that each participant received. The manual sort of standardized the way the service wanted the horses handled and gave excellent guidelines and advice. The manual also contained information on feeding, grooming, veterinary care, hoof care, anatomy of the horse and practical information. I am not sure if they still use this manual. Safety of the rider and the horse was emphasized.[148]

Banff had had a simple horse-training

well, they were ready for the trail. In Banff, this was followed by a two-to-three-day trip up the Cascade River. Pigeon adds,

Later, the Advanced Horsemanship Course was developed at the ranch, which gave the attendees more of an understanding of the mind of a young horse as opposed to older horses that had been on the trail for years. It also gave them an understanding of how the colts were trained. At the ranch the brood mares would be foaling at this time and quite often the wardens would observe a colt being born, its umbilical cord being doused with iodine and perhaps they'd observe the odd medical problem that would occur with these youngsters, i.e., scours, hernias, wind-swept legs, etc. They'd also observe the yearlings as they were tied in the barn every night. This process of putting these weanlings in the barn every night resulted in a much quieter colt. They quickly got used to humans and they knew their own stalls and what to expect – oats, hay and warm shelter.[149]

program for some years that became more in-depth after the tragic death of Neil Colgan. A similar training session was held in Jasper, as well, giving new wardens practice in grooming, saddling and packing their assigned district horses. It also included a very rudimentary introduction to shoeing horses, by practising on frozen horse hooves. At the end of the day, the newly assigned backcountry warden was given a live horse to shoe and, if all went

Pigeon enjoyed the schools, as it gave him a break from riding horses on the same trails every day that the colts quickly became familiar with. The variation in rides threw new experiences at them, which they had to learn to handle, and, consequently they became quieter on the trail.

When Pigeon took over, it was not just the warden service that was changing rapidly. As isolated as the ranch was, technology soon invaded, along with increasing levels of bureaucracy. The previously demanded business plans now came with work plans, time sheets and financial reports – all done by computer. This added far too much work to the foreman's day, but rather than hire a secretary who would probably not have the background or temperament to live on the ranch, the job was given to Debbie Pigeon. It made sense, as the foreman's job was never highly paid and the work could be done at home. Dutifully, Debbie was entered into the staff records as ranch bookkeeper. The ranch's books certainly needed improving. Hayes's records were kept on little cards that Debbie suspects he snuck into Banff to have Moe Vroom enter on the computer.

One of the biggest problems Ken Pigeon and, later, Johnny Nylund and Rick Smith constantly encountered was how to keep the ranch running with such high horse expectations when the budget was constantly examined for the smallest expenditure. The scare of losing the ranch because of budgetary concerns never left them, especially when it had nearly been lost to the Bar U Ranch a few years previously

over a budget issue. Elk and fodder were also a constant problem. The foreman always felt that the regional office and outside interests – not to mention the province – lay in wait for any excuse to dump the place. They almost snuck around, trying to make improvements without drawing any attention, scraping by on minimal expenditures.

By 1996, the Pigeons had the opportunity to take over managing the Bar U Ranch. Maybe it was Debbie looking over the fence again, an itch she seemed to get every ten years, but it was also time to get their kids into school. They had had good years at the Ya Ha Tinda and were ready to move on to new challenges. The staff at the regional office, now under Director Gaby Fortin, did not have to look far for a replacement. Johnny Nylund had been barn boss in Banff for the last several years and was pleased when he was offered the job as foreman at the ranch, a place he was very familiar with. He, too, was ready to move on.

Nylund was closely attached to the ranch and felt proud of its tradition and stubborn perseverance as a source of horses for the warden service. His special passion, however, was the horse-breeding program that was the heart and soul of the ranch. Twelve broodmares and one stallion, and the colts they produced, anchored the ranch. The colts were the real work; they were babied, gentled and trained for their destiny in the mountain parks. When Johnny and Marie Nylund arrived, they found that Pigeon had already set up a good health protocol and had the services of a fine vet. The brood mares were now mostly quarter horses, as was the registered stallion called Arrow. The horses coming out of the Ya Ha Tinda were some of the best to be found in Alberta, and Johnny Nylund decided to register the colts with the American Quarter Horse Association in 1998.

It did not take long before the Nylunds felt totally at home on the ranch, as though they had spent all their life there. Certainly, Nylund's choices in life had led them inevitably to this place. He would have to remind himself true ownership actually belonged to the government – he often felt like it was his own spread and he looked after it as if it were. If Nylund needed a reminder of that, it soon came from the Federal Heritage Building and Review Office, when the ranch qualified the old barn, built in 1942, as a Recognized Heritage Building. It spelt out loud and clear that the Ya Ha Tinda is an essential part of Parks Canada's history.

Marie soon developed a passion for the history of the Ya Ha Tinda, finding evidence of it everywhere.

When I moved to the ranch, tours of the ranch buildings had been in place to provide the public an opportunity to learn about the horse breeding and training operation and the history of the buildings, and the cultural resources found in the valley. Debbie Pigeon can tell you more about how the tours started. The tours were done by all the staff on a voluntary basis – not paid. They were basic in nature – just a quick walk through the buildings and a little history about the ranch and horse operation. It was my understanding that Ed & Judy Walker, who ran Frontier Town (now the YMCA camp) would bring their guests up to the ranch for a tour. I became very interested in its rich history from the prehistoric era, pre-contact era to the time of the Brewsters' operations, on through the years when the Ya Ha Tinda was a warden station, and later as the headquarters for the raising, training and wintering of patrol horses for the Rocky Mountains National Park. There was one small log building built in 1937 that was used over the years as a warehouse, a bunkhouse and later on as a granary. Since the building was no longer being used, I was given the go-ahead to set up an interpretive display of artifacts, objects of interest and photos of past and present life at the Ya Ha

Tinda. I volunteered to set this up and was thrilled to have been granted this opportunity and so began several years of collecting items, some of which were donated from Banff National Park. Johnny & I donated a few items as well. "Packy", the little wooden packhorse, was made and donated by Mike Schintz. He has included items in the pack boxes and it adds flavor to the tour when visitors get involved with unpacking and re-packing the little packhorse. It is fun as both the youngsters and adults enjoy tying the diamond hitch. There is a collection of photos to enhance the display![150]

Marie's interest in the history of the Ya Ha Tinda took on a new depth when she realized how important the place had been to generations of Aboriginal people as far back as the prehistoric ages. The more they rode around the ranch, the more evidence they found of these ancient societies – and, of course, there were the archaeologists who could not study the place enough. On one occasion, Johnny Nylund spotted a distinct depression in the ground that he instantly recognized as "man-made." Nothing he could think of, beyond someone digging the hollowed-out depression, made any sense. They found more throughout the prairie, some of which were grown over and appeared distinctly old. Marie told park archaeologist Peter Francis about what they had found, feeling they bore further exploration. Francis at first dismissed their finding, until Marie came across an article that described pits dug for hunting eagles found by the explorer David Thompson. The use and description of these pits were very similar to the depressions they had found. Excitedly, she pointed this out to Francis, who immediately began investigating them for himself. The conclusion was that the depressions the Nylunds had found were very old remnants of the pits described by Thompson. Marie later wrote up the discovery for Friends of the Eastern Slopes Association.

The first pit that Johnny and I found at the ranch was in the spring of 1996. Coincidentally, at the time, I was reading Jack Nisbet's book, "Sources of the River, Tracking David Thompson Across Western North America." After reading the excerpt below which is found on Page 59 of the book, I realized that this pit on the ranch was likely an Eagle Hunting Pit. Later, I found 6 more of these pits in the valley. The federal archaeologists confirmed that these are indeed remains of Eagle Hunting Pits. Originally these pits were deeper but have been blown in with soil over the years.

Incidentally, there is a nice display in the Luxton Museum in Banff of natives hunting eagles.

The natives made shallow pits which they covered with slender willows and grass under which they lay, with a large piece of fresh meat opposite their breasts; thus arranged they patiently await the flight of the eagle, which is first seen very high, scaling in rude circles, but gradually lowering, *till at length he seems determined to pounce upon the meat, his descent is then very swift with his claws extended, the moment he touches the meat the Indian grasps his two legs in his hands, and dashes him, through the slender willows to the bottom of the pit and strikes his head till he is dead. Lying in this position, and frequently somewhat benumbed, it requires an active man to pull down an eagle with his wings extended, and dash him to the ground … as the eagle never loses his courage, the whole [activity] must be quickly done, or the eagle will dart his beak in the man's face, and thus get away.*[151]

As the explorer David Thompson noted, "Some of the Eagle Hunting Pits have large flat rocks positioned on one side of the pit. Perhaps these were used in the killing of the Eagle."[152]

Once the displays were set up, Marie decided to introduce the Ya Ha Tinda to the public and soon began conducting tours through the museum and around the property. The setting alone drew many people, and she found people responded with interest in the history of the ranch.

When Debbie Pigeon started keeping the books for the Ya Ha Tinda, she was officially noted in 1994 on the payroll as "Record Keeper/Clerk." Marie had a natural aptitude for this and took over the job when the Pigeons left. It must have saved the park considerable headache, as it was necessary to keep the ranch running within budget and was way too much work for the ranch hands. The park did not want to hire an extra person, as it would mean finding additional accommodation. The work was already hampered by mail delivery that was slow and unreliable. At that time, computers were not able to handle this work. In fact, the ranch did not have computers. Communication still relied on single-side band or VHF radio – both of which were inconsistent.

Providing enough hay for the breeding stock always remained a problem, especially when the elk numbers were high. Johnny Nylund decided to keep the patrol horses on their winter range at West Lakes. To accomplish this, the Kootenay National Park trail crew was sent to build a fence on the west side of Stud Creek. Nylund notes, "Keeping the horses on this range for a few winter months helped to reduce the grazing impact by the horses on the flats near the ranch buildings and on the range on the east side of Bighorn Creek. Brush-cutting on the ranch helped to keep down the growth of willows and shrubby cinquefoil. This had been part of the ranch activities before I took on the Manager's job and I continued this program and ensured that this was done every spring."[153] Actually, planting and harvesting a hay crop was no longer part of the program. In the end, it was too much work for the results the ranch got and was only moderately successful during wet years. During the years the Nylunds lived on the ranch, the country was much too dry to produce a viable crop.

In 1999, Rob Jennings and his wife Sue, with their one-year-old daughter Shelby in tow, joined the Ya Ha Tinda staff. Rob Jennings's

background qualified him as a ranch hand, which was very beneficial for the Ya Ha Tinda over the many years he has been there. Jennings still works at the ranch, providing continuity that helps new staff grow while learning from the lessons of the past. He grew up with Parks Canada dominant in his life. His father was Hugh Jennings, who worked as a park warden in Banff for many years before transferring to Riding Mountain National Park, in Manitoba, where he retired.

In Jennings's early years, he worked on the trail crew in Riding Mountain National Park before cowboying around on the rodeo circuit. When that wore thin, he chased cows for the Prairie Farm Rehabilitation Administration on community pastures. He then pursued other work that came along, hopefully involving horses. But the Ya Ha Tinda job was "always in the back of my mind." Finally, after years spent working in the Prairies, he took a vacation in Banff and realized how much he missed the mountains. He soon found a job working for Banff outfitter Ron Warner, who owned Holiday on Horseback, which led to the opportunity to work at the Ya Ha Tinda. It was a job he had long hoped for, which provided work he loved with the bonus of steady, year-round employment.

Both Jennings and Nylund came from similar backgrounds, and they had many friends in common, so the Jennings found the ranch life an easy transition to a more isolated life. In the first few years, Shelby was too young for school, so home-schooling was not an immediate problem. However, Sue later home-schooled Shelby for Grades 1 and 2. The Jennings welcomed their daughter Jordan in January of 2003. By the time Jordan was school age, the family had purchased a small ranch near Bergen, where Sue and the kids now live while Jennings commutes to the ranch for work. The kids were free to explore their world at the Ya Ha Tinda and experience what it was like to grow up with horses. Not all of the children raised at the Ya Ha Tinda over the years took advantage of this, finding careers in other fields that had no connection with that former life. The Jennings girls, however, chose to benefit from that early exposure to horses and their father's expertise. They both continue to ride and compete in local events.[154]

Richard Levie was the third ranch hand to complete the complement of staff while the Nylunds lived on the ranch. Levie came to the ranch in the summer of 1997 with his wife Debbie and daughter Kasha. Deb was home-schooling Kasha as she completed Grades 11 and 12. Marie Nylund remembers, "Richard was a ranch hand and trained horses for us. He came from Winfield, Alberta and had been working on a community pasture and (had) experience shoeing horses. Prior to him coming to the ranch a fellow named Greg Neilson worked for the Ya Ha Tinda training horses as a ranch hand. Greg had been there for quite a few years and was a really good horse trainer. He worked for Ken Pigeon. Greg had a wife and two very small children. He left due to the issue of schooling for the kids and Richard Levie replaced him."[155]

Though life on the ranch was routine, Marie was surprised by how many unexpected events occurred over the years. A strange apparition appeared in the sky in 1997 that turned out to be the comet Hale-Bopp. It was not unique to the ranch, having been seen worldwide, but its clear skies and isolation made it spectacular to see. The second celestial event occurred a few years later, in 2001, when they "heard a sudden, prolonged, loud, rolling thunder-like boom."[156] They were still nervous after the events of 9/11, when the Twin Towers were destroyed in New York, and were actually relieved to find out it was a meteorite that fell out of the sky one afternoon. Though they did not see it, the Kootenay wardens riding in from Scotch Camp caught a brief glimpse of a flash in the sky.

In 1999, the ranch even had an airplane make an emergency landing in the flattest pasture the pilot could find below the ranch house. The pilot had left Golden, British Columbia, en route to Olds, Alberta, 37 kilometres east of Sundre, when the cloud cover trapped him and forced him down. The Nylunds watched with trepidation as he made a few passes before making a successful landing. He was a talented pilot, however, he had to wait two weeks for the right conditions to fly out under his own steam. The horses found this quite a curious new addition to their exposure to new things, and the area had to be roped off to keep them from chewing on the beleaguered plane. This, of course, happened on a day when everything seemed to go wrong. A sewer pipe had burst, flooding the basement of the ranch house, and the satellite phone antenna failed. Everything had finally been repaired just before the plane landed. At least the communication was working and they could report the incident.

The next plane to be forced down at the ranch was not so lucky. In May of 1999, Rob Jennings looked up when he heard a plane pass quite low over the ranch, heading north. It disappeared from sight, but it never quite left his mind, as the plane did not appear to be flying high enough to clear the mountains ahead of it. Jennings was not surprised to be awakened in the middle of the night by the Sundre RCMP, saying a plane had crashed northwest of the

ranch. It crashed in dense bush, incapacitating the locater signal device and it was awhile before it was found – no survivors.

The ranch also had its supply of normal wrecks from the ever-growing number of horsemen riding through the country, usually camping at the Bighorn Campground. Johnny Nylund sums up the growing use, writing,

The Bighorn Campground is a popular place, mostly with equestrians. In 1994 Banff National Park had signed a Memorandum of Understanding with the Friends of the Eastern Slopes concerning the operation and maintenance of the Bighorn Campground. A set of comprehensive rules for campground users was developed. During my seven years at the ranch the Friends of the Eastern Slopes Association were extremely cooperative and helpful in ensuring the campground was well maintained and improved upon each year. This group was comprised of dedicated volunteers who were eager to do whatever needed to be done. Hundreds of visitors, not just equestrians, visit the Ya Ha Tinda each year. Families enjoy the hike to Bighorn Falls or to Eagle Lake. The road to the ranch has been upgraded from what I experienced back in the 1960s when there were two or

three creeks to be forded by vehicle. Culverts and bridges have been installed; the road is well maintained but remains a challenge to do so – simply due to the difficult terrain in some areas. Seven Mile Hill remains the same, with its washboard and steep grade. If a person looks carefully, the old wagon road can still be seen from the top of Seven Mile Hill, where it winds down through the forest to the valley bottom. This must have been quite a challenge in the early days of wagon travel.[157]

Every other week it seemed someone had to be taken out with an injury. During the summer of 1999, STARS air ambulance had to be called out for three separate evacuations. People often went missing, requiring numerous searches by the RCMP. Sometimes members of the Ya Ha Tinda staff were recruited as searchers, but, for the most part, it did not interfere with running the ranch.

One event that proved very interesting was when White Iron Productions filmed a television series called *John Scott's World of Horses* in 1998, which featured Parks Canada's horse operation and breeding program at the Ya Ha Tinda. Two years later, Ian Tyson came for a visit to see if it was a good place to film a music video. Tyson's project did not get off the ground,

Bighorn Campground
from the air.

COURTESY MAC AND CATHY
ELDER COLLECTION.

but a few years later a location scout signed a contract with Parks Canada to produce a music video for British rock star Robbie Williams. His hit song "Feel" accompanied the western/ rodeo-themed video. The ranch yard was inundated with a film crew and all the baggage that comes with it. Daryl Hannah was the love interest, though ranch staff only caught a glimpse of her. They found it amazing how much time and effort went into such a short little video.

By 2001, the lack of fires and increasing vegetation had changed the valley from the open slopes of the late 1800s to a fairly dense forest of spruce and pine that now dominated the mountain slopes and encroached on the previously open montane meadows. There had been

no significant burning in several decades. Parks Canada and the province were just beginning a program of prescribed burns. Aboriginal people and early outfitters had historically burned off the country regularly to keep the forage and game plentiful, but that practice was abandoned decades previously after the disastrous fire in 1910. What resulted was an even greater potential for a large fire to once again burn through the eastern slopes through the aging timber. The Nylunds had already seen small fires ignite as a result of lightning strikes that were quickly extinguished, but they were occurring more and more frequently.

On September 29, 2001, the big fire finally hit. It started on Dogrib Ridge above the Red Deer River from a small tea fire that had been left smoldering. In little time it blew up into a major blaze, sending up a dark plume of smoke Johnny Nylund could clearly see from the ranch. The ranch knew that Parks Canada had begun using prescribed burns to reduce old available fire fuel around the ranch and other areas of the park. To be on the safe side, the ranch phoned in to see if this was a prescribed burn. It was not. By then, Alberta Sustainable Resource Development had been notified and an initial attack fire crew was sent in. The crew quickly put out the growing fire, but it had missed some deep smoldering duff. On October 16, temperatures climbed to 20°C, just when high Chinook winds blew over the mountains, exposing the hot embers. By mid-morning, the fire was raging again and growing fast. The fire crew was dealing not only with a wildfire in dense timber but also with unseasonably warm weather and strong winds. The fire swept across the road leading out of the ranch, cutting ranch staff off from any land evacuation. Two wardens riding out from Barrier Cabin on the Panther River caused more concern. It was thought they might unknowingly be riding directly into the path of the fire. Park wardens from Kootenay National Park had ridden in from Scotch Camp the day before and were also stranded at the ranch. The two wardens at Barrier Cabin noticed the smoke and made the wise decision to ride to the Panther trailhead, where they were eventually picked up

and taken to Sundre. Even the Mountainaire Lodge and outfitter businesses staff, along with visitors, joined the exodus. The evacuation of horses and cattle outfitters had begun.

The fire burned well into late October, narrowly missing Mountainaire Lodge. It progressed northeastwardly, just short of the small hamlet of Bearberry, before it started to slow down. But this fire was relentless. It flared up again when the wind shifted from the west to the east. Suddenly, smoke was engulfing the ranch buildings but because of the lack of visibility they could not see if the fire was headed toward them or away. The evacuation of the brood herd and other horses again seemed inevitable. But fires are monsters of unpredictability. The wind changed again and took the fire back into the mountains. When it was finally contained, the fire had covered 11,000 hectares, killing 48 head of cattle, five wild horses and countless wildlife. It had posed the biggest threat to the Ya Ha Tinda in years and stimulated both Parks Canada and various provincial agencies to work together to build firebreaks and start a more ambitious prescribed burning program for the Red Deer Valley.

Over the years, the Nylunds had many opportunities to observe the abundant wildlife that made the ranch home, either nomadically or permanently. Johnny Nylund writes,

We saw a lot of wildlife at the ranch – grizzlies, black bear, elk, moose, deer, wolves, coyotes, foxes and the odd cougar. We observed packs of up to 18 wolves. Through our spotting scope set up in our living room, on one occasion we observed several grizzlies feeding on a horse carcass in the Mare Pasture. We counted 5 grizzlies, 2 grey wolves and 2 coyotes at or near the carcass, all at the same time. The bears seemed to tolerate being in close proximity to one another and seemed to have an established order as to who fed first, second or last. The bigger bear had first right of refusal; the second largest bear was next in the pecking order. The two wolves stayed a distance away and kept chasing the coyotes away from the carcass.[158]

The biggest ongoing challenge at the Ya Ha Tinda was managing increasing human use in the valley, with the need to protect critical winter wildlife habitat and native grasslands beneficial to both elk and horses. Elk numbers and movement have, as in the past, continued to be dynamic and dramatic: from no elk at all to vast herds competing for the fescue grass. Parks Canada and Alberta Fish and Wildlife developed cooperative agreements with various universities, which found the valley was an ideal location to study elk behaviour and movement, as well as the elk's interaction with predators such as wolves and grizzly bears and people. The Nylunds soon found themselves inundated with researchers. Scientific studies have long been a priority for the warden service since the 1970s, and researchers were welcome to conduct studies out of the ranch. Johnny Nylund writes, "Several studies were going on during the time we lived at the ranch. Mark Hebblewhite was doing studies on wolf, elk and forage for the University of Alberta. Mark and his team spent a lot of time at the ranch studying various elk and wolf behavior linked to such things as migration habits, predation, elk forage, populations including birth statistics and survival rates. The University of Alberta students studied the rough fescue grass as well. I believe these studies might still be in progress with long term monitoring."[159]

When Parks Canada became an agency under the Parks Canada Agency Act in 1998, it was removed from any department, gained a CEO and lost ministerial protection.[160] Prior to this, our national parks had been addressed under several names in their hundred-plus-year history. "The governing body that represented Parks Canada was established on May 19, 1911, as the Dominion Parks Branch under the Department of the Interior, becoming the

Elk with cut block for elk graze in background.

world's first national park service. Since its creation, its name has changed, known variously as the Dominion Parks Branch, National Parks Branch, Parks Canada, Environment Canada – Parks Branch, and the Canadian Parks Service, before a return to Parks Canada in 1998."[161] Former Chief Park Warden Perry Jacobson had this to say about parks becoming an agency: "In my mind agency was a bad idea and Parks Canada is still suffering from the decision. For example it promised that there would be more autonomy at the Park level when it fact the power base shifted to Ottawa to maintain control. Revenue was supposed to stay mostly in the Parks but that did not happen. The switch to an Agency caused a lot of headaches for the warden service as this was the start of reorganization and the warden service and Interpretive Service seemed to be the main target. It didn't have much of an effect on the Ranch."[162]

Once again, the political changes at the upper echelons of government had no immediate effect on how the Ya Ha Tinda was run. The subtle but significant change meant that Parks Canada no longer had the responsibility of a government department. Rather, it was now an agency, which meant it had become a business operation and had to be run as such. Funding to keep our national parks running had to be generated within the national parks, just like any other business. How well this would work and the effect it would have on the Ya Ha Tinda did not manifest itself during the period the Nylunds spent managing the ranch. They enjoyed a particularly quiet period, free from the threat of annexation from other governments, agencies or outside interests. Their welcome mat was always out and the ranch, particularly the horse program, flourished under Johnny Nylund's tenure as ranch manager. He retired in 2003, leaving with reluctance but confident the Ya Ha Tinda would survive as a horse ranch for the foreseeable future.[163]

Warden leaving the Ya Ha Tinda in the spring with his district horses.

PHOTO BY BRADFORD WHITE.

Warden riding back to the Ya Ha Tinda in the fall.

PHOTO BY BRADFORT WHITE.

CHAPTER 6
THE SHIFTING SCENE

Living as we do in the present, we do not realize that there is no present, only a shifting scene
that is not two days the same and that all we know today may be and will be gone tomorrow.
—Louis L'Amour, *Education of a Wandering Man*

When Marie and Johnny Nylund left the ranch in 2003, the Banff administration decided to hold a competition for the job of ranch manager.[164] Formal hiring procedures took the place of appointments and the ranch foreman position (now called ranch manager) went to competition in keeping with the hiring practices for the rest of Parks Canada. This was the first time the job had come up for competition, as opposed to appointing government personnel with past horse experience who worked up to the position. A number of people applied, but the job went to Rick Smith, a local cowboy who was working for the Brewster outfitting business in Banff at the time. Both Rob Jennings and Richard Levie competed for the job, but only Jennings stayed on after the competition. Levie wanted a future – he did not feel the job

of ranch hand at the Ya Ha Tinda promised this and left soon after.

Once again, the cost of running the ranch was reviewed, but now the breeding program came into question. The warden service was in turmoil at the time, and it was uncertain how many horses would be needed, with cutbacks coming to the backcountry staff. A close look at the breeding program convinced Resource Conservation Manager Ian Syme that it was too expensive to maintain, and it was scrapped in favour of buying horses at auction.[165] The sale of the broodmares was a decision made by the Banff Field Unit under Syme. There should not have been any question as to the quality of horses the ranch was turning out, but it did take a big investment in time. During the hiring interim, the task of selling off the mares

The centennial ride.

and colts was given to warden Bradley Bischoff, assigned to act as temporary ranch manager.

When Rick Smith took over the job full-time in 2003, the practice of buying older horses was already in place. It was a particularly hard blow to the Nylunds, who felt the heart of the ranch was in the breeding program. They had worked hard at turning out great horses and were very proud of this accomplishment. At least Marie was able to buy one of the mares she particularly favoured.

For Smith, the manager job at the ranch was a new experience. He was one of the few foremen who had not worked there previously in one capacity or another, though he knew the place well. Smith elaborated on this, saying,

> *Jean and I knew the ranch a little bit. Jean had been through the ranch on hiking trips and we'd camped at the Bighorn Campground quite a few times in the past. I had come out of the park [Banff] a lot with pack trips and we'd started our trips here or end them here so I knew Slim Haugen and Cal Hayes and all those guys. Most of the guys that worked at the ranch in those days ... Steve Bennett and Ken Pigeon ... were friends of mine that I'd worked with in outfitting. So the move up here wasn't that big of a challenge. The first thing when I got the job I think I woke up on the floor kind of surprised that that had happened. We had to sit down and pinch ourselves and say, "We really are going there to live!" That was a big change. But when we got here we were lucky. For the first year or two, it took just learning the routines, the different seasons, what was expected of you, how the whole place operated from generators to the water system to everything else. In those days it was a pretty isolated place. We had one satellite phone that was expensive and awkward to use most of the time.*[166]

Rick and Jean Smith brought a fresh vision of how the ranch should be run. Change was coming, though it was not obvious where that would lead in the coming years.

As far back as 1998, wardens with an astute insight into the future saw that turning Parks Canada into an agency boded ill for the warden service. And anything that affected the warden service ultimately had repercussions at the Ya Ha Tinda. It actually did not have an immediate effect on the ranch at the time, but the future changes affecting the warden service's status would.

The warden service was under the umbrella of a government union, the Public Service Alliance of Canada (PSAC), and it found a vocal voice in Doug Martin – a representative for the warden service currently involved in a strike action over the use of hand guns. Most of the warden service was actually exempt from this action, as they were deemed an essential service. Everyone else was pressured to strike. Martin was not thinking when he found out that the staff at the Ya Ha Tinda refused to join in the strike action. His thoughts must have been clogged with visions of the union winning its grievance when he drove out to the ranch to persuade the cowboys to quit working and honour the strike. He probably convinced himself that the ranch was so isolated, the staff did not know about the strike or that they were expected to participate. The result was foreseeable to anyone who knew Cal Hayes. One dark (and soon to be stormy) night, Martin knocked

on Hayes's door and proceeded to instruct him on what the PSAC expected of them. Ken Pigeon happened to be there at the time and recalls, "I can't believe how rude he [Cal] got. It was right now and he said, 'These damn horses don't give a shit what you do or whether you strike. They need to be fed and to be fed every day. You can get in your truck and get off this ranch now!' And he meant it. He was instantly fired up and he was mad."[167]

Martin had a thick skin and retreated to the confines of the Banff warden office to soon take up another cause dear to the heart of some law-enforcement-prone wardens. Unfortunately, this would be the catalyst for the ultimate disbanding of the warden service. When the warden service was created in 1909, it was the intent of Howard Sibbald that the wardens would have the powers of law enforcement officers and were sworn in as peace officers. How else could they enforce the National Parks Act in the far-flung wilds delineated by boundaries that traversed vast icefields, bush-bound forests and remote, high-alpine meadows that sheltered the now endangered caribou and grizzly bear? They were not, however, issued handguns, as it was not deemed necessary for their type of work.

But as visitation increased and more confrontational situations occurred, wardens prone to law enforcement felt handguns were required for on-the-job protection and took the problem to the PSAC. Parks administrators fought this idea tooth and nail. They could not see the friendly park warden, whose principal job was firefighting, wildlife protection and public safety, armed with guns, despite the hat badge and flashes indicating they were also officers of the law.

But there were bigger issues with the warden service fomenting in Ottawa long before the gun question came to a head. Due to its primary role in conserving park natural and cultural resources, the warden service had a significant influence in regulating commercial development and operations within the national park. If there was any conflict between development and habitat conservation, the warden service provided important input to park managers on whether the project went ahead or went ahead with mitigations. This sometimes became a thorn in the side of the development-conscious administration, which had the additional mandate to treat national parks as a business that needed to make money. The warden service was seen as gaining too much influence and, as a consequence, began to develop opposition in Ottawa. Again, Perry Jacobson had his ear to the ground.

The issue of guns and the Union was the biggest factor, but it goes back farther than that period. When I was acting Superintendent at Kootenay National Park in the mid 1990's I had access to a couple of options that were being considered by the Superintendents that were designed to break up the Warden Service into various components. In fact it was during that time when ecosystem management was turned over to a different administrative section. I think the union and a few strong advocates for guns, played right into the hands of senior management. As you know I have always ranted on the issue, but it's only speculation on my part and not proven. Also reorganization leaned toward specializing wardens, which was the end of a multitasked group that wardens were so well respected for.[168]

The reorganization of park wardens accelerated as specialization needs increased to handle a range of tasks formerly handled by the warden service functioning under one hat. In larger parks, this was especially true, as responsibilities encompassed wildlife management; fire management; search and rescue; resource protection, including environmental assessments, cultural resource protection and community outreach; and law enforcement. A whole lifetime could be spent becoming competent in each of these fields alone. Smaller parks with minimal staff continued (and, to a large extent, still do today) to share the workload if it did not exceed their training or manpower. If a major event occurred, such as a large, out-of-control fire or a complicated rescue, help from the larger parks was forthcoming. The downside was reducing the warden service's ability to protect the park as a whole. While these essential areas of responsibility were being beefed up across the country, the former skills of the backcountry warden were slowly eroding. The role of the generalist, multi-skilled warden was already unravelling when Rick Smith took over the Ya Ha Tinda in 2003.

Rob Jennings noticed changes on the ranch soon after Smith became foreman. He observed,

There have been a lot of changes; some positive; some negative I guess. The horse program is run a lot different than when I first started at the ranch. Mostly out of necessity. The park staff as a general rule have changed a lot; there are a lot more seasonal staff and a lot less people with horse backgrounds so this means that the horses have to be even quieter than they were before. And the people need instruction so we do a lot of horse schools to teach new

people. When John Nylund retired Banff shut down the breeding program much to everyone's chagrin. They thought they could buy horses cheaper than raising them. But the turnover (of horses that did not work out) has been too high. We have (since) gone to buying weanling colts.[169]

Smith instructed Jennings and the other ranch hands to continue to train and supply horses to the warden service as had been done in the past, but he increased the amount of training both horses and wardens received. The new warden staff had very limited exposure to horse use and more advanced training was required before the staff felt these new employees were safe to travel on their own. This was also true of the horses. Because they were going to less experienced people, it was felt the colts needed at least another couple of years of training at the ranch before being assigned to a particular park or person. This required keeping the colts on the ranch until they were four to five years old. In the past, it was normal to send them out as three-year-olds, though they still had a lot to learn on the trail. This worked well when the wardens knew enough to continue on-the-job training but could be disastrous when the men or women were greener than the horses they got. Once Smith and

Jennings realized this, a second advanced class was added. This had the advantage of reducing the potential for accidents, but it seriously cut into the amount of time the district wardens could spend in the districts they were assigned to. Instead of getting out early on the trail to address the work needed to keep the districts running smoothly through the summer, the wardens were spending that time at the ranch learning to ride and care for their horses.

However, by 2007, the warden service had to deal with a devastating development that far exceeded any backcountry problems. The ongoing issue of gun armament for the warden service would ultimately lead to the end of the service, as it had been known until 2008. In 2008, Labour Canada ruled in favour of the PSAC arming the wardens with handguns for law enforcement. Parks Canada had fought this ruling but finally capitulated, with the stipulation that only wardens engaged in law enforcement would be armed. (Prior to this, all wardens were sworn in as law enforcement officers, regardless of their current duty, and could enforce the National Parks Act wherever and whenever it was breached in a national park.)

To accomplish this, management split the former warden service into three branches: Resource Management, Public Safety (mountain rescue) and Law Enforcement. It also deemed law enforcement a singular specialty, requiring extensive training. Because of the cost, only a handful of former warden employees were selected (60 in all of Canada), and only those would retain the title of "park warden." The warden "service" was gone. The specialized wardens would be fully armed and identified with park flashes and badges, while the rest of the former park wardens were given a nonspecialist uniform that identified them only as park employees. The new fully trained park wardens, equipped with badges, guns, nightsticks, bear spray and heavy vests, report only to Ottawa. Former wardens now work for a resource conservation manager in separate specialized units mentioned previously. Understandably, the chief park warden is long gone.

The disbandment of the warden service as an entity in Parks Canada was merciless, sudden and devastating. It happened in May 2008, well remembered by the wardens attending an advanced horse school at the Ya Ha Tinda, where the weather more than mirrored the shocking news. It was snowing heavily, making for very difficult conditions to run a school, and some participants even considered heading home early. Before anyone left, a phone call to Bill Hunt (current resource conservation manager of Banff) – who was at the ranch that day – brought a quick end to the training. With disbelief, all those in attendance were told they were no longer wardens and had to immediately divest themselves of anything that indicated their former status as peace officers. That meant removing badges, flashes and any identifying truck decals. The red and blue truck lights even had to be taped and covered before they could leave the ranch. But it was not just the ranch that received this directive. Similar action was being taken in the national parks all across Canada. That cold night at the ranch was the first of a long wake, mourning the loss of a once substantial and effective unit that had previously protected the parks with dedication and zeal. It was a confusing and disheartening period for most employees until their new status was clarified.

Though this did not immediately affect the number of "resource management specialists" from patrolling the backcountry, Rick Smith saw problems on the horizon. The Ya Ha Tinda was there to provide horses for the warden service. Without the warden service, it became a question of who would be using the horses. Smith soon began to investigate the other options for horse use. As Rob Jennings put it, "You can't have horse power without man power."[170]

Though the new ranch manager started the job facing these unforeseen challenges, Smith states, "Well, we didn't make changes right away and some of it was kind of put upon us. When I first got here the ranch taught only one horse course a year and it was called an Advanced Horsemanship Course. It was five days and there might be five or six people. With changing from the old service to the more modern service, we got a lot more staff with no background in horses at all. The original park wardens had some background in horses [but now] we had to step up our training and our teaching a whole bunch from days gone by."[171]

He explains further,

And then there are other things besides the horses. The people (Parks Canada staff) are so green that we had to change our whole horse-training program. Instead of riding colts for six months and turning them over to the older Parks Canada staff who would take them over, now we have to bring the horses into the parks ready to go pretty much for anybody. So our training of the horses has changed. And now we have an arrangement with Olds College where they (farrier students) come out once a year. It is great for the students as we have 60 or 70 head of good broke, quiet horses that they

*can trim and it helps us to get the horses
ready for the spring. We do all of our worm-
ing and inoculations that day, and trim all
the horses' feet as well. Also we brand if it is
necessary. We work with all sorts of different
groups out here. It has been on-going and it
changes every year.*[172]

The necessity to work with other people and agencies became more pressing when
Parks Canada slashed the jobs of government
employees all across Canada in 2012 – mostly
without warning and with little to no notifica-
tion. It happened on one particular day in late
April, now referred to as "Black Monday." It
was not restricted to the warden service alone;
huge cuts came for staff in all departments of
the federal government. People were called into
the office they reported to and told to see their
immediate employer. When they left, a few
sported half-smiles of relief to still be working
(while never certain for how many months of
the year), while many went and picked up their
belongings and left for good. The employees at
the ranch were equally uncertain about their
jobs and the future of the ranch. To Rick Smith's
relief, all of the staff stayed on, with the only
change being a cutback to the number of hours
Jean would be employed. Jean adds, "I was the
only one affected at the ranch by the cutbacks.

I was cut back to 0.25 and it was decided that
I would get paid for half days for six months,
then be laid off for 6 months. Of course, the job
didn't go away, just the pay cheque."[173]

Miraculously, the Ya Ha Tinda was not lost
and the focus of supplying horses to the western national parks continued as before. At that
point, Glacier National Park was no longer
using horses and Yoho's and Kootenay's horses
were kept at Lake Louise. (Yoho now keeps up
to seven or eight horses in the park). The number of horses wintering at the ranch dropped
from a high of 250 head to 100 head at the low-
est. With Parks Canada's demand for horses significantly lowered, ways of keeping the ranch
solvent had to broaden. Smith soon found out
that other people were interested in what the Ya
Ha Tinda had to offer.

*We were approached by the military
(Department of National Defense) a few
years ago and it was the Special Operations
Forces that were taking climbing courses
through Parks Canada already. Then they
heard about the horse program and they
thought they could use this training for
search and rescue, overseas deployments
and things like that. So we set up a course for
them and they usually come every year, or
every two years, whichever works for them.*

They [are usually] here for two weeks. They pay per person, per day and that includes their accommodation, the training and the use of the horses and equipment. So it helps the ranch (financially) in the long run. We also winter horses for the Alberta Parks Service with the provincial government. And we contract one 3-day horse school for them in the spring. And they pay as well, so that helps foot the bills at the ranch. Fish & Wildlife and the R.C.M.P. have used the ranch for different courses here. So it isn't strictly Parks Canada staff. Anyone that is in the federal or provincial governments that needs some horsemanship training or support.[174]

Other ongoing sources of horse use and revenue at the ranch are the ecological research and restoration programs originally set up to study the migration and impact of elk on the ranch habitat. The federal government originally established these programs in the 1950s. By the 1970s, the work was continued by provincial biologists and researcher Luigi Morgantini from the University of Alberta. This was later expanded in the 1990s by Professor Evelyn Merrill, also from the university, Cliff White, Banff's ecosystem research manager, and provincial biologists Eldon Brun and Jim Allen.

In 2008, the University of Montana joined the research group led by Professor Mark Hebblewhite, who had previously studied wolf and elk movements in the valley for several years. The Alberta and federal governments, and many other granting agencies, now fund these long-term, innovative projects. Following the example set by Morgantini to use horses to track migrating elk, horse involvement in the research program has grown significantly.[175]

Using horses to haze elk off the ranch seemed to work well when researchers tried to force the elk to migrate back to their traditional summer range in the park. Once researchers were given permission to use the government horses, the training of green staff took on a whole new dimension. It started slowly, but soon the benefits of using horses for many applications of research began to grow. So did the enthusiasm of the students using the horses. Smith is keen about the students using the horses, finding it a great benefit to the horse's exposure to new situations and new people. He can now say, "The researchers that we get here are in a partnership between the University of Alberta, the University of Montana, Alberta provincial biologists and Parks Canada. We get the benefit of all the knowledge they gain through their research. They are a great bunch of kids, a good bunch for our program too because they use horses for a lot of it especially for this last elk project. It's good for us as we work on our training skills working with them and they are using horses and we can get the young horses used to strangers a lot quicker. All and all, it has worked out very well."[176]

Though, in some ways, Rick and Jean Smith do not have the deep ties to the warden service that many former ranch managers (foremen) had, they knew enough about the changes to realize that former wardens were seeing the end of an era. This became abundantly clear when they saw the effect Black Friday had on the wardens attending a horse school at the ranch that day. As mentioned previously, the wardens were told to remove all vestige of uniform indicating they had any connection to law enforcement. They also had to cover up (duct tape) truck decals declaring they were park wardens and even tape over the red and blue lights. Everyone reacted differently, but mostly with disbelief. Disheartened, the former wardens returned to their designated offices of employment in the various parks to learn their fates.

Early suspicion that the days of the warden service as a multitask function of the park service were ending prompted the formation of warden alumni in 2004 for retired park wardens. The Park Warden Service Alumni Society's goal is to maintain the spirit of what the service once stood for. As such, its aim is to retain the history and values of the former warden service by documenting its oral history and sponsoring special events. The alumni wanted to expand this role to volunteer work within the various parks and providing mentorship programs, but the restriction placed on them by Parks Canada was too onerous to get any of this work off the ground. In the end, the warden alumni did what was possible within the limitations of what was permitted. It organized a party. The year 2009 marked the 100th anniversary of the inception of the warden service and the best excuse possible to say goodbye to a way of life.

To celebrate the anniversary, a large celebratory party was organized for the summer of 2009, to be held in Banff National Park. Part of the program, which ran over two days, involved a commemorative ride from the Ya Ha Tinda to the town of Banff, otherwise known as party central. The ride actually took three days, mirroring the horse drives of the past, when the horses were returned to Banff in the spring. It was a huge event involving 28 riders and 38 horses. It was also a very emotional event that both Rick and Jean took part in. If they had any doubts about the place the Ya Ha Tinda had in the heart of the warden service, it was dispelled on that ride. Jean said,

I think that ride was very important to everyone who participated. And, from the response on Banff Avenue when we rode in, I think it was important to the whole warden centennial. The response from all of the people watching was emotional you know. And I think that everybody knew that the warden service was forever changed. This was a way to show the pride for a job well done. The feelings, the emotions, the story telling and everything that happened on that trip was very up-lifting and I think that we felt it was a real privilege to be along on that ride because we felt everything that everybody else felt. It was really important to get some closure on the change that was happening to the wardens.[177]

Art Laurenson, a warden who had worked in various capacities over the years, best describes the ride in his entry in the Stoney Creek Cabin journal. He titled it, "The Journal Entry in the Stoney Creek Backcountry Warden Cabin Banff National Park September 11, 2009." Laurenson wrote,

There wasn't very many of us in this country. It started with a handful of roughriders and others on the fringes of the law whose nefarious activities became official when fire and game guardian status was bestowed upon their trusty souls in 1909. Nevertheless, something drew them to the task, men with hard shells and soft souls; they loved what they did and pursued it with passion and bottomless love – the preservation of some dotted lines on a map called Banff National Park. Counting a century on in time now countless boots and horseshoes have made their mark and yet never faded away. A collective memory remains, couched in stories told around campfires and cook stoves, that maintains the mystic and magic of being a national park warden. The reality of lives risked, and lost, amidst bears, horses, floods, fires, and avalanches is lost on most who will never see this country through passionate eyes.

So it is with tremendous pride that twenty-eight of us, with some 520 years of service, mark the Warden Service Centennial by riding from the Ya Ha Tinda to Banff. Yet another page of prints pounded into the storybooks we call trails. Today, we ride down Banff Avenue, back into "civilization" and a new and uncertain world for the warden service. Regardless of the change, reorganization, policy, directives, and politics, this century old family will ride through it, persevere, and prosper for another hundred years and lay down many not-so-tall tales on dusty trails for our future family to remember and celebrate.

The new norm at the ranch was now working with horses bought at auctions (or other sources) and training green people from functions or organizations, including and in addition to park staff. But the cutbacks to the warden service did not bring a significant change to running the ranch. "We didn't notice much of a change at all out here. We still had the same job to do, the same colts to train, the same amount of (or maybe more) people to teach horsemanship to, the same amount of feeding and care of the stock, the same amount of maintenance and the same amount of fencing, etc."[178]

As with any ranch, however, the safe rule is to expect the unexpected. Since the early years of fire suppression, both the national parks and the province have had an ongoing battle with fire control as old-growth forests develop, supporting a growing layer of duff that is classic fuel for large fires. This recognition has led to controlled burns both in the parks and the province. Smart fire practices are being employed to protect towns and structures from potentially large fires by clearing the underbrush and building fireguards. Controlled burns help to reduce old-growth forests, which can fuel very large fires over considerable hectares. Though

the Ya Ha Tinda is technically in the province, it is still federal surface property and the responsibility of Banff National Park to protect. The park's fire resource specialist for many years was Ian Pengelly. In 2009, Pengelly's crews and contractors logged close to the ranch to create a fuel break in preparation for the prescribed burn the following year. They waited until conditions were just right to create a good, tight, hot burn. But fires are even more unpredictable than the weather, which ultimately controls what happens to a fire. On this occasion, the wind unpredictably turned, sending the raging blaze toward the buildings on the ranch. For a few mind-twisting days, the firefighters fought an uncontrolled burn that ate up several acres of trees not meant to be burnt as it headed for the ranch. They got it under control and finally out before any damage was done. Smith adds, "We'll never forget it and certainly learned a lot from it."[179] Now, when you ride over the hill from the ranch buildings, a great swath of burnt trees greets the eyes. But as with most fires, it is a part of the ecological cycle of the mountains and will soon support the prairie grass that grew there in the early years of the ranch.

Though there were changes in the horse program, it was less a radical change than a shift of emphasis. The ranch hands spend

more time training horses and people than in the past, but the regular work of maintaining fences and feeding and caring for stock has not changed. When circumstances dictate, ranch staff still invites the public to tour the historic display and answers questions about the ranch, though staff members try to post these times for groups rather than individuals. They also remain closely connected to the Bighorn Campground and the Friends of the Eastern Slopes Association, which looks after it. Smith elaborates, saying,

Yeah, we do have a great relationship with them and it has been going on for a long time through Johnny (Nylund) and Ken Pigeon and ever since they started. The "Friends" are a huge asset as they take care of the day-to-day maintenance of the washrooms, gravelling roads, and building high lines and tie stalls. They even have a "host" that helps people with trail conditions and advice on where to go and what to see and things like that. The public being able to use the ranch here has always been welcome. They have always been able to hunt on most areas of the ranch. We keep one area, our pastures, where they are not allowed in and they have been good about that. There are a lot of people who love to come out and

ride. Parks Canada has never charged anybody for this and for the use of the land. And so, to have the "Friends" there and through donations they tend to the maintenance on the trails and in the campground and all that has been fantastic. We get an average of 9,000 horse nights [number of horses kept in the campground] a year down at the campground and that is all walks of life … people from as far away as Vancouver Island. Mostly they are Albertans but we've had people from Quebec and Ontario with their horse trailers and their horses. I think it is a really good thing and it is a really good thing for Parks to keep it; something that people can afford to do and enjoy their horses and camp with their families.[180]

The Friends of the Eastern Slopes Association is precisely what it says it is. It is a not-for-profit society that was incorporated in 1994, with the primary objective of providing stewardship for the Bighorn Campground at the Ya Ha Tinda. Becoming established as a recognized society, with the responsibility for the campground and the others that followed, was initially quite a challenge. In 1993, the Bighorn Campground was in poor shape and considered poorly located by Parks Canada, its custodian. Up to that point, this campground was a popular

staging area for trips to the Ya Ha Tinda and surrounding country, particularly for hunting in the fall. But what made it most attractive was there were no camping fees. That summer, the multiple users were alarmed when the campground was closed by parks due to a bear problem (probably connected to poor garbage control). There was also a rumour floating around that parks intended to close the campground permanently in 1995, after negotiating with the provincial Department of Fish and Wildlife to open a new campground at Eagle Lake. The new site was on higher ground, close to the old campground, but it had limited vehicle access. The province also decided to hand over the operation of the campground to a private company that would charge campground fees – the price to be set by the company given the concession. Clarence Stewart, a local rancher and big user of the park campground, helped organize a meeting with local hunters, campers and backcountry users at Mountainaire Lodge to discuss the problem.

The problem was considerable. Parks Canada was responsible for its upkeep, but whether due to not charging fees or just no interest, the campground had few facilities. The people who had attended the meeting formed a loose group, with Stewart as spokesperson, and requested detailed information from the regional office,

which at that time was managing the Ya Ha Tinda. They received a letter from the Calgary regional office, stating, "In recent years the area has gained considerable popularity and the number of recreational horse users has increased dramatically. As a result there is considerable environmental damage at this facility. What is needed is outhouses, bear-proof garbage containers, feed-proof storage facilities, water wells, hitching rails, firewood supplies." Also mentioned in the letter was the issue of the creek freezing to the bottom every winter, forcing water and ice into the campground area. The letter went on to state, "To meet the needs of recreational horse users Parks Canada has begun negotiations with provincial authorities to develop a more suitable facility just east of the Ya Ha Tinda Ranch. The Eagle Creek facility is scheduled to be available for public use in the fall of 1995 at which time camping on the Ya Ha Tinda Ranch will be discontinued."[181]

Armed with this knowledge, a meeting with 150 people in attendance was held in Innisfail, Alberta, on February 5, 1994, to sign a petition to keep the campground open (the petition was eventually signed by 3,300 people). At this time, the Friends of the Eastern Slopes Association (FOES) was formed and Clarence Stewart became the president. What followed was a series of meetings with the superintendent of forestry from Rocky Mountain House and Parks Canada (with Doug Stewart from the regional office) to see if all three interest groups could come to a solution.

Other political bodies became embroiled, but, finally, the nitty-gritty issues were resolved between parks, forestry and FOES. Not surprisingly, it was a matter of cost. Pit toilets were no longer acceptable to Alberta Lands and Forests, especially as they were located too close to a significant water source. They had to be replaced with fibreglass holding tanks that were costly both in purchasing and in maintaining. The commitment of FOES suddenly became real and substantial. Stewart recalls, "During our lunch break our executive agreed that each of us would contribute $200 out of our own pockets. So we went back to this meeting and we said, 'Okay guys, we are buying the new (toilet) tanks.' The club (FOESA) had about $800 at that time and the executive members' personal contributions of about $1,200 covered the cost. So that kind of sealed it at that point. So then, we discussed further what we were going to do. We purchased the tanks for $1,942.00 and they were installed on August 15th, 1994 and they were operational for that weekend. So that kind of sealed it."[182]

But, as First Nations people had learned years earlier, verbal agreements with the government (provincial or federal) are not always binding. FOES tried to set up a memorandum of understanding between it, Parks Canada and Alberta Forestry to take over and run the campground under the provisions stated in the memorandum. FOES thought the matter was settled until it discovered one of the officials with forestry would not sign, as he was opposed to the presence of horse manure. But FOES was lucky. The regional office was downsizing in 1995, and it gave the management of the ranch back to Banff National Park. Charlie Zinkan, then superintendent of Banff, gave the Ya Ha Tinda portfolio to Perry Jacobson, superintendent of Kootenay National Park, because of his strong background in ranching. From then on, the negotiation came down to two parties, allowing an agreement to be reached that gave the stewardship of the Bighorn Campground to FOES. It appears Banff felt no need to involve the province if all pollution concerns were addressed. From that point on, the care and upkeep of the campground under the watchful eyes of FOES has more than met any government standards. The spirit of cooperation between reasonable people allowed a volunteer organization to maintain and uphold standards in a large popular campground that was so poorly run by the federal government prior to its involvement.

As Rick Smith stated, FOES has done a phenomenal job of this after signing a memorandum of understanding with the Parks Canada Agency. FOES currently maintains a membership of over 400 families that live on the periphery of the mountains and have a lifelong commitment to the welfare of the land. Its success convinced Alberta Sustainable Resource Development and the Bighorn Backcountry Committee to add the stewardship of the Hummingbird, Eagle Creek and Cutoff Forest recreation areas to its sphere of monitoring and protection. This has resulted in a real reduction in the impact on the environment of recreational horse users.

FOES' dedication was never more evident than when the unprecedented Alberta flood hit the campground in June 2013. Smith remembers the change in weather happened violently in the space of a few hours: "I heard the weather change in the middle of the night and by 6 am the bridge over Bighorn Creek had water flowing about a foot below the bridge."[183] When it became evident the campground, people, trailers and livestock were in danger, everyone pitched in to save what they could. The ranch staff worked with several volunteers from FOES and work crews from Clearwater County to move everyone to higher ground before the main deluge of water swept everything away.

One of the main problems the volunteers and work crews had was reaching the campground, when the only access road was threatened by the raging Red Deer River. Fortunately, the ranch staff could drive to the campground and were able to help as soon as the water began to rise. Rick Smith's description of the event leaves little doubt it was quite a fight.

Half of the campground was already completely under water and we started moving people up to the north end (of the campground) and then we just got them partially moved and we had a bit of a berm built to keep the ground from flooding during the winters and that washed out and all of a *sudden two-thirds of the campground was up to your waist in raging water. It was unbelievable. It just about washed away some horse trailers. We managed to get a hold of them and got them pulled up on higher ground. We had a pretty expensive haystack, yard down here – we had big $300,000 motor homes and 5th wheels and all kinds of stuff parked there for a while.*[184]

Many people recall the near disaster the flood almost caused that June day. Jean commented, "Once the bulldozer got in and made a trail, anyone with a reliable vehicle … would take other people and their horse if they didn't have a vehicle that they thought they could get through with. So they commuted out in a convoy behind the bulldozer. If there was a problem, the bulldozer could pull them out." Dale Marshall from FOES recalls, "We had a cat and a Shell grader and operator. The ranch used their tractor and Tim Barton was there with his tractor. We picked up the logs that had washed up and they were used to level out and fill in other areas. We also rebuilt some roads."[185]

Though Clearwater County was always good at helping with the road in an emergency, maintenance of the only vehicle access to the ranch was an ongoing concern. Even while the Smiths were there, the road had frequently become

impassable for various reasons: loss of culverts, shifting land or just plain wear and tear. After the 2013 flood, Parks Canada realized that significant repairs were needed and the personnel at the Ya Ha Tinda are hoping this will happen in the near future.

Though no lives or horses were lost or hurt in the flood, accidents do occur on occasion. But Jean Smith is amazed at how many things happen that individuals solve themselves. She recalls one time hearing of a man being swept over Bighorn Falls and bystanders jumping in to save him. Again, FOES always seems to be there to lend a hand to those in trouble. In fact, the ranch staff often sees helicopters coming in to pick someone up who may have signalled for help with a SPOT device or a cellphone.

Even the most experienced person can have an accident when horses are involved. On one memorable occasion, Jean's horse spooked and started running away with her. "It happened so fast, before I could pull him up, he stumbled and threw me off. I ended up with a plate and 11 screws in my shoulder. But I was riding with three of the best guys that I could have been riding with … and that was Ian Pengelly, Cliff White and Rick Smith."[186] What amazed all of them was how quick the response was from Parks Canada, which sent in a helicopter within the hour that whisked her away to the hospital and straight to emergency. On another occasion, Rick Smith spent the night under a cliff high on a scree slope with an injured rider. It rained most of the night, but the man survived and was safely rescued the next morning. All part of the job as Smith sees it.

The fact that the ranch today is connected by such advanced communication to the busy hubbub of urban resources still astounds the staff because of how quickly the change happened. Jean is more aware than the others of the rapid changes, as her job requires constant communication with the main office. She adds, "Well, we are totally 'plugged in.' So, all the changes within Parks Canada, with timesheets, with leave requests, everything to do with Pay & Benefits or H.R. [Human Resources] is on-line now. We are responsible and contribute in our way as well. So, [the main office] has set us up with new technology and Parks Canada – Banff – you know … we are not way out here and forgotten anymore."[187] The ranch even has big screen TV and can get a multitude of channels. With the recent improvement to the road, it only takes 2.5 hours to drive from the ranch to Cochrane, significantly reducing the sense of isolation so prevalent in the past.

Despite the accessibility and the increased usage by riders and hikers, the wildlife still retains a foothold on the land. This varies most dramatically with the elk, but as Smith observes,

Yeah. They have been on the decline for quite a few years. You'd read back in history in the early 1990s, guys would say there was 2,500 elk here. Now, whether that was true I don't know for sure. When we came here there were about 1,200 head and it declined to a point where there was about 350 head. Through some information that we have learned from the researchers, if an elk herd has a calf survival rate in the first year of over 25 percent, then the herd is growing, and this herd has been. According to the researchers this herd has a 25 to 27 percent elk survival rate. That has brought our herd back to – I think the count last spring was around 500 head so it is going in the opposite direction again, which is nice because with a 10,000 acre ranch and our horse herd down in size, we need the elk and the deer to graze this land off or it becomes a fire hazard.[188]

Rob Jennings adds,

Cliff White predicted that the ranch could handle about 300 head of elk in the wintertime. The interesting thing is that in the last 6 years that is basically the number we have observed on the ranch. It seems to be

quite balanced – the grass is better. Some of the other animals have come back in stronger numbers – like the mule deer and a lot of white tail deer – way more than we used to have. There seems to be hundreds of deer here now. A lot of people think the elk died off. I don't think that they did; I think that they have just moved elsewhere. There has been a lot of logging in the province that has created new habitat for the elk.[189]

Mark Hebblewhite studied the fluctuation in elk population at the Ya Ha Tinda, noting a distinct change in migration behaviour over the years. He was able to distinguish between elk that remained on the ranch year-round versus elk that migrated to the high alpine meadows deeper in the park for richer summer graze. Basically, elk staying on the ranch did so to avoid predation during migration from wolves and grizzly bears. The hay put out for the horses became a supplement for the elk, enticing them to stay year-round. After studying the increase in wolf population, and the effects of prescribed burning, which should enhance elk forage, Hebblewhite states conservatively that resident elk tend to fare better than those that migrate to summer pastures.

The high numbers of elk observed in the 1980s "occurred after a series of intermediate precipitation summers and immediately after fires in Banff National Park and winter range enhancements," such as clearing land and putting out hay for the horses. In Hebblewhite's opinion, this was not a sustainable number for the available forage and the subsequent decline was predictable.[190] The study of elk dynamics affected by predation, migration, prescribed burning and human interaction is ongoing with Evelyn Merrill from the University of Alberta.[191] It is a complex interaction that is not easily understood without years of comparative studies, particularly with sudden and radical climate change altering the environment.

According to Rob Jennings, the deer are still in abundance but so, too, are the wild horses. The feral horses are a contentious issue with local ranchers but are still considered wild animals by the Alberta government. At present, they can be found in healthy numbers on the approach to the ranch from the east. Jennings sees them often while driving to work, noting, "The other thing that is interesting to me when I drive out to the ranch Monday mornings from Sundre at this time of the year is that I'll see the wild horses a lot more. The population is expanding. It is a lot heavier than what the government horse population is out at the ranch. I noticed that the elk seem to follow the wild horses around and whenever I run into wild horses I also run into elk. They seem to have a symbiotic relationship and there seems to be more elk where the wild horses range."[192]

An abundance of game should attract carnivores, though neither Smith nor Jennings specified seeing an abnormal number of cougars, wolves or bears preying on the elk herd that uses the ranch. Cougars are thought to be still abundant, but these elusive animals are hard to count. The biggest asset provincial and parks wildlife biologists have in determining the population movement and number of wary predators is the monitoring cameras set up on game trails. Banff National Park usually has about five active wolf packs, with two or three of these packs sometimes hunting in the ranch area. Former Chief Park Warden Ian Syme noticed their presence on the ranch while visiting shortly after being promoted to the job in 2001. He recalls, "When the wolves came back, they just showed up at the ranch – not due to any specific park management – though carnivores had not been hunted for some time in national parks."[193]

Additional wolf packs use the province's Bighorn Wildland. Monitoring shows that grizzly bears are relatively common in this portion of the eastern slopes, and they are managed with strict regulations to minimize human-caused bear mortality.[194] The research programs set up to study the interaction of predator – prey dynamics have occurred fairly recently in a historical time continuum that has a very shallow database, making it difficult to see the big picture for the future, as the fluctuations in elk populations demonstrate. The same could be said for buffalo, except that human occupation of the land has effectively eliminated their original range.

For nearby Banff National Park, bison restoration is now ecological, legal and a political priority. Archaeological and historical evidence indicates they were a pervasive and deterministic presence in the eastern slopes of the Rocky Mountains, and especially the nearby Great Plains. The role of bison goes back thousands of years, being especially important to the traditional lifestyle of First Nations people. Some of the oldest evidence of buffalo is present in long-forgotten Aboriginal campsites found on the Ya Ha Tinda. The grasslands have some of the highest densities of old wallows anywhere in the Rocky Mountains. These were made when mixed groups of bulls and cows met here each summer to mate. Both the bulls and cows rolled in the soil, creating the large, dish-shaped indents found abundantly on the ranch. These haunting remnants of the past are now grown over with grass but not hidden from those who look. Former Banff National Park warden and biologist Cliff White, aware of the archaeological, historical and ecological evidence supporting the use of the front range of the Rockies by buffalo, sees no reason why they should not once again return to their historical habitat: "As happened with bringing back elk in the 1920s, the national parks can work out the kinks of bison restoration techniques within the confines of Banff's valleys. Likely, recreational hunters will eventually see the benefits of these restoration efforts – just as they have for many decades since parks brought elk back to the eastern slopes."[195]

This is a contentious program, as the migratory nature of bison has made previous efforts to reintroduce them to the mountain national parks less than successful. In past experiments, mature bison were brought into both Banff in the 1920s and Jasper in the 1970s, but they soon escaped, to the immense displeasure of local ranchers. However, Parks Canada has continued to redefine techniques and is now a world leader in bison reintroductions. In the last two decades, now using young animals with fewer "homing instincts," bison from Elk Island National Park have been successfully reintroduced in Russia, Alaska, Saskatchewan and Montana. Moreover, a joint research article by Parks Canada staff and the University of Montana and its College of Forestry and Conservation indicates concern over the future of the buffalo, or, more accurately, the plains bison: "In Canada, plains bison are threatened, occupying less than 0.5% of their former range."[196] It is recognized that farming, ranching and fencing makes natural migration impossible. The better scenario would be to reintroduce the bison into a habitat that is historically natural to them yet provides the protection they need while minimizing their tendency to migrate.

However, as Cliff White points out, one site recommended by the researchers is in Banff National Park.

Banff National Park is recognized as historical range of plains bison and has been identified as a potential site for the reintroduction of a wild population. Park Managers need to recognize that centuries of hunting by Blackfoot, Salish, Kootenai and then the Stoneys made the continental divide the western edge of bison range. In the past, in most years, there were likely only a few dozen bison in the area of Banff Park itself, maybe at most a hundred or so. They were easily hunted as you go further up narrow mountain valleys. Restoring ecological integrity to Banff, both scientifically and legally, requires only a few small herds

*of wary bison. More is not better. The feds
don't need to risk winter bison stampedes
down the streets of Sundre or Canmore.*[197]

It has taken some years to get this project
off the ground, but it is now in full swing. The
first bison will be located in the Panther and
Cascade river valleys – a two-day's wander to
the Ya Ha Tinda for the large animal. In fact,
the Ya Ha Tinda is currently one of the cen-
tres of operation for the project. In 2016, four
young bison were brought to the ranch, where
they are now held in a fenced enclosure to condition the horses to their presence. Though
Rob Jennings laments the decrease in horse
use from what it once was, he sees the bison
project as a benefit for horse use on the ranch:
"The bison project will use horses and Karsten

Heuer, who is the project manager, is sending his people that will be working with the bison project, up to the ranch to get trained with horses. It will be the only management tool the team will have once they start releasing the bison."[198]

Rick Smith and his staff at the Ya Ha Tinda hope the federal government will take an active interest in the horse ranch as a function to provide well-trained people and horses. This may, in turn, promote continued upkeep of backcountry trails and facilities in mountain national parks. The elimination of the park warden service has left the backcountry vulnerable to deterioration of its facilities and an increased potential for poaching. Arguably, this reflects Canada's changing culture. We have become more of an urban society, with a growing immigrant population that has not inherited the traditional values of the old rural West. In short, the cowboy with a ranching history, the outfitter, the hunter and the general outdoorsman are becoming a thing of the past. The skills necessary to run a ranch, raise a mountain-wise horse, hunt big game or even travel safely in the backcountry are being eroded rapidly. Finding people to replace the present staff, who have years of experience training backcountry horses, will become a challenge. Even finding older horses that can be

trained properly for this work is getting harder and harder. Smith is skeptical of the success of the horse-buying program, with its poor rate of return. A lot of time is spent going to auctions and private sales, trying to buy a horse that looks good but turns out to be unsuited for the work – and the cost is increasing rapidly. Smith laughs when he reflects on how difficult it can be to judge a horse's capacity at a private sale or auction: "I don't know if people really lie to you but they definitely don't know what they are talking about quite often, when they tell you how great some of these horses are. And then you bring them home and find out … 'Wait a second that's not the same horse I was talking to him about.'"[199]

Rob Jennings added to this later, saying, "You won't find a good horse at an auction, and when you do find one, they are very expensive."[200]

Though it is unlikely Banff will re-establish the breeding program, it is now doing the next best thing: buying weanlings at much cheaper prices. It is easier to teach a horse properly when they are young than to buy one burdened with baggage from previous owners. Smith explains,

We started out thinking we'd buy two and three year olds that were un-broke but it didn't take us too long into our program to

learn that we couldn't find many that other people hadn't tried to start and the reason that they were at the (horse) sales was because they had tried and failed and those horses came with a lot of baggage.

As it was, we were lucky if 50 percent of them worked out to what we wanted for Parks Canada horses. And so, we decided about three years ago to buy weanlings, bring them home, halter break them, trim their feet and everything and bring them in the barn for the first year and get them going good and then as two-year-olds we'll ride them half a dozen times and turn them out again. As three-year-olds they come into the barn and they begin a two-year training program that will school them for backcountry trips with different crews and this kind of thing and get them used to other people. By (the time they are) five years old we are hoping they are ready to go to the parks. I think it is going to be a whole lot more successful because these horses have been started from the ground up with our program and the same program we are teaching everybody who comes to school here. The two barn bosses [from Banff and Jasper] teach as well. So all of us are on the same program, and the horses are on that program and the people coming up are on

that program and it works. I think it is going to work like gangbusters.[201]

This pleases many of the wardens who have been involved with the ranch over much of its history. It is a warden home and has been celebrated on any occasion that warrants a get-together. The main events have been two reunions that few can forget. Marie Nylund kept details of the work that went into the success of these occasions, citing support from people and organizations.

The first Ya Ha Tinda Reunion was held on Saturday, June 7, 1997 at the ranch. If I recall correctly there were 310 people who attended this celebration. Tickets were sold in advance.…

The second Ya Ha Tinda Reunion was held on Saturday, June 12, 2004 with just over 200 people in attendance. The event was organized by Jim Murphy, Scott Ward and other members of the Banff Warden Service Social Committee. The weather was very wet, however it did not stop those in attendance from having a great time. Again a pig roast was provided for dinner. There was also an afternoon entertainment program, sales of memorabilia, books, t-shirts, baseball caps etc. A cash bar was provided as well. The Wardens Band was hired to

Rick and Jean Smith at the new dedication plaque celebrating 100 years of the Ya Ha Tinda Ranch. Plaque donated by Park Warden Service Alumni Society.

PHOTO BY DON MICKLE.

provide the music for the dance. Again, tables, chairs, festival tents and portable toilets were rented for this event. Parks Canada again supplied the dance floor, tents and equipment such as generators, BBQs and pancake grill etc. A pancake breakfast was provided with volunteers from Banff National Park cooking and serving.

The volunteer support from Parks Canada was essential in making these events such huge successes.[202]

With the bison project underway, the horse requirement seems likely to increase. Indeed, Jean Smith notes, "Banff is actually short of horses ... they need more. We have given them three or four colts this year that the boys [horse trainers] have just finished [training] and Banff could still use a couple more. With the elk monitoring and the Bison Project and everything else going on ... they are starting to use the horses much more extensively. And the two-man trail crews are really starting to step up their horse use again too, which is great."[203]

The year 2017 marks the Ya Ha Tinda's 100 years of existence, with all its trials and tribulations, as the only working government horse ranch in Canada. The continued future of the ranch at this centennial moment of celebration seems bright. In Rick Smith's opinion, there are good reasons to justify Parks Canada having retained the ranch, running just as it is now: "In my opinion the ranch is justifiable for many reasons: Training centre for Parks Canada horses, horsemanship training for Parks Canada staff, revenue generated from other government departments such as Department of National Defense, Alberta Fish & Wildlife

and Alberta Parks; public appreciation, historical, its ecological and cultural value; a buffer to Banff National Park; a wildlife research centre; and a staging area for bison reintroduction." He realizes it is not an easy job and that the ranch must eventually be run with people who can make decisions, have an independent yet flexible spirit and not mind the isolation. Rick and Jean Smith certainly have found that, but, more importantly, it is a place that must be set in the heart. Smith reflects,

Well, I am sure that every ranch manager that has been here has had different things that the times have dictated to them and you just go with the flow. You have to learn to be pretty versatile here because you are not sure what the next e-mail is going to bring you. You have to be ready and prepared for things like the bison project, etc. You know, we heard about it for years and then all of a sudden 'bang' we are going [with the bison project]. *And so, it is time to get your hands out of your pockets and get going.*[204]

His is a good attitude to have in the rapidly changing atmosphere of politics in Canada and the unforeseeable outlook the next generation will have. At present, there is even a movement afoot to reinstate the ranch into Banff National Park. Would this be positive or negative? Bill

Hunt, the current manager of resource conservation in Banff National Park, who is responsible for the ranch, is skeptical. To him, it brings up a number of problems that could lead down a complex number of paths. Parks Canada's relationship with the Province of Alberta seems to be at a comfortable status quo and there are no other outside interests vying for the land. But that could change in a heartbeat. Perhaps some unknown precious metal is hidden in the gravelly depths that will become indispensable to Canada's economic future. Perhaps the Brewster family will find a long-hidden document that will give them an undisputed claim on the land. But for those who have called the Ya Ha Tinda home, even long before it became an official horse ranch for the Government of Canada, it is a root that runs deep. The ranch is a home place that has no equivalent, a Shangri-La of the heart.

If you want to go fast – go alone
If you want to go far – go together
—African Proverb

Acquainting horses and buffalo at the Ya Ha Tinda 2017.

ACKNOWLEDGEMENTS

I would first like to thank the Park Warden Service Alumni Society executive for its dedication to the Ya Ha Tinda book project for its 100-year celebration as a government horse ranch in support of Parks Canada operations in the national parks of western Canada.

Specifically, grateful thanks go to the president of the alumni society, Dale Portman, for his unwavering support and aid in research and reviewing of the book as it was being written. It would have been a daunting task without his encouragement and help.

I must also thank the book committee for reviewing and adding documents from several sources now difficult to find. I would like to thank Marie Nylund for her input and patience in this regard. Her attention to small details and unique interviews were invaluable to this book, as well as her personal photographs.

Cliff White, Rod Wallace and Dave Reynolds were particularly helpful in reviewing and editing the first draft, which had to be completed in a short period of time. Cliff provided his unique knowledge of the ranch – its vegetation and wildlife history, as well as an understanding of how a story should be told. Rod contributed to the flow of the document and the importance of what should be included, which indicated how truly he understood the significance of the ranch and its horses. I would like to thank Dave for his editing skills and dedication to ensuring that the book was well documented. I would also like to thank Don Mickle for being an invaluable source of information and stories and for responding enthusiastically to constant questions to which were given prompt answers.

I must also thank Rick and Jean Smith for their enthusiasm and openness to seeing the book written and for allowing me access to the ranch itself. The time spent with them was extremely informative to conveying the later years of the Ya Ha Tinda and the direction they wish to see it take.

Finally, thanks to the many who helped behind the scenes and contributed to the project – it could not have been done without the support given in innumerable ways. I must also thank those who provided me with their photographs for use in the book, in particular, Bradford White. However, my most profound thanks go to the warden service itself for the wonderful work done by this branch of Parks Canada in protecting our national parks over the last 100 years, working tirelessly to protect the boundaries of these precious lands. May you forever be Ya Ha Tinda bound.

DONORS

In 2016 and 2017, the below listed donors supported two legacy projects launched by the Park Warden Service Alumni Society. One of the projects was the creation of a cairn with a bronze plaque, celebrating the Ya Ha Tinda's 100th anniversary, which has been erected right in front of the manager's house on the ranch, next to the Canadian flag. The other project is this book, *Ya Ha Tinda: A Home Place*. I would like to thank the people and organizations that made these legacy projects possible:

Gordon Anderson

T.S. Anderson

Gord Antoniuk

Peter Applejohn

Rob Ashburner

Colleen Balding

Lawrence Baraniuk

Rick Blackwood

Doug Burles

Alfie & June Burstrom

Brian Carleton

Dorothy Carleton

Michael Carleton

Terry Carleton

Dave Carnell

Frank Coggins

Madeline Crilley

Lorne & Shirley Cripps

Terry & Marie Damm

Perry Davis

Ann Dixon-Bruder

Peggy (Dixon) McRae

Bill Dolan

Doug Eastcott

Mac Elder

Tom Elliott

Ray Frey

The Friends of the Eastern Slopes Association

Mike Gibeau

Larry & Jane Gilmar

Smokey & Lynn Guttman

Bob Haney

Larry Harbidge

Dennis Herman

Alice Hermanrude

Robert Hermanrude

Jack Holroyd

Beverly Hunter

Perry Jacobson

Greg Keesey

Greg Keesey in memory of Doug Anions

Linda Kraft

Rick Kunelius

Eric Langshaw

Garth Lemke

Colleen Loxam and family

Sid Marty

Alan McDonald

Kevin McLaughlin

Don Mickle

Al Moore

Jim Murpy

John & Marie Nylund

Glen Peers

Ian Pengelly

Jim Purdy

Jim & Ruth Quinn

Dan Reive

Bob Reside

Colleen Reynolds

David Reynolds

Gordon Rutherford

Neil Schroeder

Brian Sheehan

David Skjonsberg in memory of Earl Skjonsberg

Terry Skjonsberg in memory of Earl Skjonsberg

Greg Slatter

Cyndi Smith & Peter Achuff

Al Stendie

Bob & Erla Stevenson

Cynthia Stewart

Ian Syme

John Taylor

Michel Vallee

Bill Walburger

Rod Wallace

The Wardens Band

Don Waters

Rob Watt

Dennis Welsh

Alan Westhaver

Bradford White Photography

Cliff White

Max & Julie Winkler

Chris Worobets

The Park Warden Service Alumni Society also thanks the Province of Alberta for a research grant received from the Historical Resources Foundation, Heritage Preservation Partnership Program funded by the Alberta Lottery Fund.

Letters of support for the grant application were received from The Whyte Museum of the Canadian Rockies, Stockmen's Memorial Foundation, Cochrane Historical Society, Sundre Historical Society, Parks Heritage Conservation Society and the Friends of the Eastern Slopes Association.

YA HA TINDA BOUND

There's a place on the eastern slope, in the mountains deep
It's a place of rolling grass where the Red Deer River sweeps
I'm riding north into that land where silence can be found
I'm riding north, I'm Ya Ha Tinda bound

In Canada, the Great White North, the bitter cold descends
Alpine passes choke with snow and Mother Nature sends
A bitter wind down valleys steep chills me to the bone
I'm riding north, I'm Ya Ha Tinda bound

These ponies they deserve a rest, been going hard since June
Step out son, it's not far now, we're gonna be there soon
These horses tend to slip and slide and skid on frozen ground
I'm riding north, I'm Ya Ha Tinda bound

When I arrive, I'll pull their shoes, and turn 'em out on grass
They will lope out through the gate, they are free at last
When heavy snows obscure the ground they'll feed on bales round
I'm riding north, I'm Ya Ha Tinda bound

I see the ranch past Wardens Rock as vistas open wide
My pace picks up, this is the end of a long and cold hard ride
When spring arrives we'll chase 'em in and trailer them to town
After six months' work they'll be Ya Ha Tinda bound

The boys at the ranch, they train these colts from good range stock
They'll gentle 'em and ride 'em hard till they don't shy or balk
When these colts go to the parks, they'll be good and sound
After six months' work they'll be Ya Ha Tinda bound

When I'm old and crippled up and can no longer ride
I will sit out on my porch and remember those vistas wide
And when it's time to bury me beneath the cold hard ground
In my mind I'll be Ya Ha Tinda bound

—Scott Ward

NOTES

Chapter 1: Discovery

1   F.O. "Pat" Brewster, *Weathered Wood: Anecdotes and History of the Banff-Sunshine Area* (Canmore, AB: Altitude Publishing, 1977).

2   O.P. Dickason, *Canada's First Nations: A History of Founding Peoples from Earliest Times* (Toronto: McClelland & Stewart Inc., 1992).

3   P.D. Francis, "End of Season Report" (Ya Ha Tinda Ranch Archaeological Services, report on file with Parks Canada, Calgary, 1993), 6.

4   E. Luigi Morgantini, "The Ya Ha Tinda: An Ecological Overview" (Canadian Heritage, Parks Canada, 1995), 48.

5   Cliff White, personal communication with author, 2017; Clifford A. White, *Bison Movement Corridors in the Western Cordillera, North America: 2017 Progress Report* (Canmore, AB: Canadian Rockies Bison Initiative, 2017).

6   Morgantini, "The Ya Ha Tinda," 49.

7   Brewster, *Weathered Wood*, 9.

8   Ian A.L. Getty, "Stoney-Nakoda," *Historica Canada*, http://www.thecanadianencyclopedia.ca/en/article/stoney-nakoda.

9   Raoul R. Anderson, "Alberta Stoney (Assiniboine) Origins and Adaptations: A Case for Study," *Ethnohistory* 17, no. 1 (Winter-Spring 1970): 49–61. Available historical information is sketchy, imprecise and somewhat speculative, but it leads to certain interesting and still researchable tentative conclusions. In his unpublished studies of the Alberta Stoney, John Laurie gives historical and ethnological data that lead him to propose that they may have been in the foothills west of Edmonton by about 1650 or even earlier; John Laurie, "The Stoney Indians of Alberta," vols. 1 and 2 (Glenbow Foundation, Calgary, AB, 1957). A mid-17th century entry into the area would roughly coincide with the westward push that presumably began in about 1670, as both groups, equipped with firearms, moved to participate in the fur trade. See John C. Ewers, *The Blackfeet: Raiders on the Northwestern Plains*, The Civilization of the American Indian Series, vol. 49 (Norman: University of Oklahoma Press, 1958); John C. Ewers, "Was There a Northwestern Plains Subculture? An Ethnographical Appraisal" *Plains Anthropologist* 12, no. 36 (May 1967): 167–174.

10 Anderson, "Alberta Stoney," 58.

11 Ted Binnema and Melanie Niemi, "'Let the Line Be Drawn Now': Wilderness, Conservation, and the Exclusion of Aboriginal People from Banff National Park in Canada," *Environmental History* 11, no. 4 (2006): 726.

12 Morgantini, "The Ya Ha Tinda," 49.

13 Brewster, *Weathered Wood*.

14 Hugh A. Dempsey, *Indian Tribes of Alberta* (Calgary: Glenbow-Alberta Institute, 1979).

15 Ted Byfield, ed., *Alberta in the 20th Century*, vol. 1, *The Great West before 1900* (Edmonton: United Western Communications Ltd., 1991), 63.

16 Binnema and Niemi, "'Let the Line Be Drawn Now,'" 726–727. The CPR was also important because it promoted the establishment of Canada's first national park. That the early histories of national parks in Canada and the United States are so similar is unsurprising because the national parks movement in the United States directly influenced Canadian decision makers and the public. William Pearce even used some of the wording of the act that created Yellowstone National Park and the regulations for the Arkansas Hot Springs when he drafted the Rocky Mountains Park Act of 1887.

17 Sid Marty, *A Grand and Fabulous Notion: The First Century of Canada's Parks* (Toronto: NC Press Ltd., in cooperation with Cave and Basin Project, Parks Canada, and the Canadian Government Publishing Centre, Supply and Services Canada, 1984), 37.

18 Morgantini, "The Ya Ha Tinda."

19 Robert J. Burns, with Mike Schintz, *Guardians of the Wild: A History of the Warden Service of Canada's National Parks* (Calgary: University of Calgary Press, 2000), 3. Historian E.J. Hart, in *The Brewster Story: From Pack Train to Bus Tour* (Banff: Brewster Transport Company, 1981), recorded, "In May 1901, Bill (Brewster) fortunately obtained the position of forest ranger and game guardian for Rocky Mountains Park. The regulations of 1889 prohibited the shooting, capturing or killing of wild animals in the park and the taking of fish by any means other than rod and reel. Limited manpower at Superintendent Stewart's disposal weakened the enforcement of the regulations."

20 Marty, *A Grand and Fabulous Notion*.

21 Burns, with Schintz, *Guardians of the Wild*, 3. "In April 1907, Douglas hired a Chief Game Warden, Philip A. Moore, and argued for more stringent firearms and poaching regulations."

22 Brewster, *Weathered Wood*, 11.

23 Ibid., 12.

24 Ibid., 10.

25 Ibid., 11.

26 C.J. Taylor, *Parks Canada's Ya Ha Tinda Ranch: A History* (Calgary: Western Canada Service Centre, Parks Canada, 1999).

27 Binnema and Niemi, "'Let the Line Be Drawn Now,'" 738.

28 Ibid., 737.

29 Burns, with Schintz, *Guardians of the Wild*, 736.

30 Ibid.

31 Taylor, *Parks Canada's Ya Ha Tinda Ranch*, 4.

32 Ibid.

33 Marty, *A Grand and Fabulous Notion*, 90.

34 Taylor, *Parks Canada's Ya Ha Tinda Ranch*, 6. It is interesting that, despite all these conflicts,

Howard Sibbald's daughter Adele married Jim Brewster, later giving her name to Dell Valley, a popular ski run at the then Brewster-owned Sunshine ski area near Banff. Cliff White, personal communication with author, 2016.

35 Marty, *A Grand and Fabulous Notion*, 100.

36 Ronald Spadafora, *McGraw-Hill's Firefighter Exams* (New York: McGraw-Hill Professional, 2007), 230.

37 Jack Fuller, *Red Saddle Blankets* (self-published, 1980), 92.

38 Muriel Eskerick, *Road to the Ya Ha Tinda: A Story of Pioneers* (self-published, 1960).

39 Taylor, *Parks Canada's Ya Ha Tinda Ranch*, 6.

40 Ibid.

41 Brewster, *Weathered Wood*, 11–12.

Chapter 2: The Golden Years

42 Susan Feddema-Leonard, *People & Peaks of the Panther River & Eastern Slopes* (Grande Cache, AB: Willmore Wilderness Foundation, 2012), 8. The following is an excerpt from an interview by Feddema-Leonard with Bud and Annette Brewster:

> *Sue:* From what you have shared, the Brewsters were using the Ya Ha Tinda area for a long time. I found out in my research that Bill and Jim Brewster applied for a lease in 1904 and that the application was approved in 1905 under the name Brewster Brothers Transfer Company. It appears from what you have discussed today that the Brewsters had been using the area for many years prior to that. Records show that the Brewsters were finally forced off the Ya Ha Tinda in 1917 and the documents cited many different reasons regarding the revocation. There appears to have been a tug of war during the next half century between the federal and provincial governments over the right to control that land base. Common sense might suggest that the Brewsters should have had some kind of rights considering their historic use, similar to squatter's rights.
>
> *Annette:* Well yeah but I don't think that was even implemented in those days. Nobody even worried about that [rights]. You were just there using the land. Then I suppose time went on. R.B. Bennett and the [federal] government were trying to implement things. That is how the government got involved. The whole process came apart and we were restricted to use that area we call the Company Ranch (Now Meadow Creek off the Trans-Alta fire road up the Ghost River).

43 Taylor, *Parks Canada's Ya Ha Tinda Ranch*.

44 Colonel F.J. Scott, "Wild Horse Roundup at Ya Ha Tinda" (unpublished memoirs, Glenbow Archives, 1967).

45 Fuller, *Red Saddle Blankets*, 95.

46 Ibid.

47 Scott, "Wild Horse Roundup at Ya Ha Tinda," 1.

48 Fuller, *Red Saddle Blankets*.

49 Anne Dixon, *Silent Partners: Wives of National Park Wardens* (self-published, 1985).

50 Fuller, *Red Saddle Blankets*, 104.

51 Scott, "Wild Horse Roundup at Ya Ha Tinda," 4.

52 Fuller, *Red Saddle Blankets*, 92.

53 Morgantini, "The Ya Ha Tinda," 6.

54 Burns, with Schintz, *Guardians of the Wild*.

55 Taylor, *Parks Canada's Ya Ha Tinda Ranch*.

56 Ibid., 12.

57 Marty, *A Grand and Fabulous Notion*, 98.

58 Taylor, *Parks Canada's Ya Ha Tinda Ranch*.

59 Ibid., 20.

60 Nellie Murphy, "A History with National Park Wardens, 1919–1950" (unpublished manuscript), 22.

61 Burns, with Schintz, *Guardians of the Wild*.

62 Murphy, "A History with National Park Wardens," 23–24.

63 Ibid.

64 Ibid., 70.

65 Anne Dixon, oral history, Park Warden Service Alumni Society, 2012.

66 Burns, with Schintz, *Guardians of the Wild*, 96. McTaggart-Cowan later wrote,

> It is most unfortunate that it seems to be so difficult to get the Warden Service, and in some cases the local administrative staff, to realize that they are not running a game reserve but supervising a National Park. The gamekeeper attitude of immediate antipathy towards any carnivore will keep cropping up. Perhaps … we can legitimately hope that the time will arise when the reaction to situations such as this will be "Here is something that needs study" rather than the current reaction of jumping to immediate conclusions and going for a gun.

67 Taylor, *Parks Canada's Ya Ha Tinda Ranch*, 23.

68 Ibid., 25–26.

69 Ibid.

70 Randy Mitchell, "Banff National Park Warden Service during the 1940s (as seen through the daily journals kept by Bruce Mitchell, Chief Park Warden, 1941–1949)" (Whyte Museum of the Canadian Rockies Archives, 2006), 4.

Chapter 3: An Uncertain Future

71 Morgantini, "The Ya Ha Tinda."

72 Burns, with Schintz, *Guardians of the Wild*, Appendix B.

73 Taylor, *Parks Canada's Ya Ha Tinda Ranch*.

74 Ibid., 28.

75 Dixon, *Silent Partners*, 13.

76 Ibid., 14.

77 Morgantini, "The Ya Ha Tinda," 28.

78 Ibid., 30.

79 Ibid.

80 Dixon, *Silent Partners*, 10.

81 Ibid., 23.

82 Ibid., 19.

83 Evelyn Gilmar, oral history, Park Warden Service Alumni Society, 2015.

84   Letter from Shirley Cripps to the Park Warden
     Service Alumni Society, 2016.

85   Ibid.

86   Ibid.

87   Ibid.

88   Don Brestler, *Face into the Wind* (self-pub-
     lished, 1999), 6.

89   Ibid., 50.

90   Ibid., 52.

91   Ibid., 53.

Chapter 4: Some Degree of Settlement

92   Taylor, *Parks Canada's Ya Ha Tinda Ranch.*

93   Georgina Campbell, "The Horses of Canada's
     National Parks," *Canadian Horse Journal*
     (March/April 2001): 32.

94   Don Mickle, "The Ya Ha Tinda: A Historical
     Working Ranch, Heritage Area Plan" (1998).
     Ray Legace, from Lake Louise, and Jimmy
     Simpson, from Bow Lake, who had lifetime
     grazing rights at Tyrell Creek, grazed horses
     south of the ranch.

95   Murphy, "A History with National Park
     Wardens," 78.

96   Bruce Mitchell, "Suggested Improvements
     in the Warden Service Organization" (Banff
     National Park, 1944, 1959), 45.

97   Burns, with Schintz, *Guardians of the Wild*,
     Appendix B.

98   Taylor, *Parks Canada's Ya Ha Tinda Ranch.*

99   Burns, with Schintz, *Guardians of the Wild*,
     Appendix B.

100 Mac Elder, personal communication with
     author, 2016.

101 Feddema-Leonard, *People & Peaks*, 414–415.

102 Ibid., 415.

103 Mac Elder, oral history, Park Warden Service
     Alumni Society, February 19, 2011.

104 Taylor, *Parks Canada's Ya Ha Tinda Ranch.*

105 Mickle, "The Ya Ha Tinda," Appendix B, 567.

106 Don Mickle, "My Friend Ben" (unpublished
     memoirs, 2006), 6–8.

107 Colleen Hayes, personal communication with
     author, 2016.

108 Evelyn Gilmar, oral history, Park Warden
     Service Alumni Society, 2015.

109 Colleen Hayes, personal communication with
     author, 2016.

110 Brestler, *Face into the Wind*, 57.

111 Feddema-Leonard, *People & Peaks*, 268.

112 Ibid.

113 Lorne and Shirley Cripps, interview by author,
     2016.

114 Lorne Cripps, oral history, Park Warden Service
     Alumni Society, 2015.

115 Don Mickle, personal communication with
     author, 2016.

116 Ibid.

117 Dale Portman, personal communication with author, 2016.

118 Christine Cripps, email to the Park Warden Service Alumni Society, 2016.

119 Taylor, *Parks Canada's Ya Ha Tinda Ranch*.

120 C.A. White, D.D.B. Perrakis, V.G. Kafka, and T. Ennis, "Burning at the Edge: Integrating Biophysical and Eco-Cultural Fire Processes in Canada's Parks and Protected Areas," *Fire Ecology* 7 (2011): 74–106.

121 Dickason, *Canada's First Nations*.

122 Taylor, *Parks Canada's Ya Ha Tinda Ranch*.

123 Burns, with Schintz, *Guardians of the Wild*.

124 Kathy Patterson, personal communication with author, 2016.

125 Gaby Fortin, personal communication with author, 2016.

126 Kathy Patterson, personal communication with author, 2016.

127 King was a ranch hand at the Ya Ha Tinda from 1982 to 1986. Brian King, personal memoirs, Park Warden Service Alumni Society, 2016.

128 Oak Plested, personal communication with Marie Nylund, 2016.

129 Ibid.

130 Taylor, *Parks Canada's Ya Ha Tinda Ranch*.

131 Perry Jacobson, personal communication with author, 2016.

132 Taylor, *Parks Canada's Ya Ha Tinda Ranch*, 35.

Chapter 5: Resolution to an Elusive Future

133 Dale Portman, personal communication with author, 2016.

134 Gaby Fortin, personal communication with author, 2016.

135 Taylor, *Parks Canada's Ya Ha Tinda Ranch*.

136 Perry Jacobson, personal communication with author, 2016.

137 Taylor, *Parks Canada's Ya Ha Tinda Ranch*, 36.

138 Perry Jacobson, personal communication with author, 2016.

139 Gaby Fortin, interview by Dale Portman, 2016.

140 Ken and Deb Pigeon, oral history, Park Warden Service Alumni Society, 2016.

141 Ibid.

142 Ibid.

143 Mac Elder, personal communication with author, 2016.

144 Burns, with Schintz, *Guardians of the Wild*, 258–260.

145 Sid Marty, *Switchbacks: True Stories from the Canadian Rockies* (Toronto: McClelland & Stewart, 1999).

146 Perry Jacobson, personal communication with author, 2016.

147 Ken and Deb Pigeon, oral history, Park Warden Service Alumni Society, 2016.

148 Marie Nylund, personal communication with author, 2016.

149 Ken and Deb Pigeon, oral history, Park Warden Service Alumni Society, 2016.

150 Johnny and Marie Nylund, oral history, Park Warden Service Alumni Society, 2012.

151 Jack Nisbet, *Sources of the River: Tracking David Thompson across North America*, 2nd ed. (Seattle, WA: Sasquatch Books, 2007), 59.

152 Marie Nylund, personal communication with author, 2016.

153 Johnny and Marie Nylund, oral history, Park Warden Service Alumni Society, 2012.

154 Rob Jennings, oral history, Park Warden Service Alumni Society, 2016.

155 Marie Nylund, personal communication with author, 2016.

156 Johnny and Marie Nylund, oral history, Park Warden Service Alumni Society, 2012.

157 Ibid.

158 Ibid.

159 Ibid.

160 Taylor, *Parks Canada's Ya Ha Tinda Ranch*.

161 Claire Elizabeth Campbell, ed., *Century of Parks Canada, 1911–2011* (Calgary: University of Calgary Press, 2011), 1.

162 Perry Jacobson, personal communication with author, 2016.

163 John Nylund, oral history, Park Warden Service Alumni Society, 2012.

Chapter 6: The Shifting Scene

164 Ian Syme, personal communication with author, 2016.

165 Ibid. At the time the ranch was looking at cost-cutting measures, the average price for buying a good, well-broke horse was low. Considering the time needed to be invested in training colts to a higher standard, it seemed much more economical to buy older horses.

166 Rick Smith, oral history, Park Warden Service Alumni Society, 2016.

167 Ken and Deb Pigeon, oral history, Park Warden Service Alumni Society, 2016.

168 Perry Jacobson, personal communication with author, 2016.

169 Rob Jennings, oral history, Park Warden Service Alumni Society, 2016.

170 Ibid.

171 Rick Smith, oral history, Park Warden Service Alumni Society, 2016.

172 Ibid.

173 Jean Smith, personal communication with author, 2016.

174 Rick Smith, oral history, Park Warden Service Alumni Society, 2016.

175 Cliff White, personal communication with author, 2016.

176 Rick Smith, oral history, Park Warden Service Alumni Society, 2016.

177 Jean Smith, personal communication with author, 2016.

178 Rick Smith, oral history, Park Warden Service Alumni Society, 2016.

179 Ibid.

180 Ibid.

181 Clarence Stewart, interview by author, 2016.

182 Ibid.

183 Rick and Jean Smith, oral history, Park Warden Service Alumni Society, 2016.

184 Ibid.

185 Personal communication between Rick and Jean Smith and Dale Marshall, 2016.

186 Jean Smith, personal communication with author, 2016.

187 Ibid.

188 Rick Smith, oral history, Park Warden Service Alumni Society, 2016.

189 Rob Jennings, oral history, Park Warden Service Alumni Society, 2016.

190 Mark Hebblewhite, personal communication with author, 2016. Hebblewhite observed that elk fare less well in new burns when wolves are present.

191 Mark Hebblewhite et al., "Is the Migratory Behavior of Montane Elk Herds in Peril? The Case of Alberta's Ya Ha Tinda Elk Herd," *Wildlife Society Bulletin* 34, no. 5 (December 2006): 1280–1294.

192 Rob Jennings, oral history, Park Warden Service Alumni Society, 2016.

193 Ian Syme, phone interview with author, 2017.

194 Cliff White, editing notes, 2016.

195 Cliff White, discussion at a Park Warden Service Alumni Society meeting, 2016. See Cliff White et al., "Plains Bison Restoration in the Canadian Rocky Mountains: Ecological and Management Considerations," *Proceedings of the George Wright Biannual Conference on Research and Resource Management in National Parks and on Public Lands* 11 (2001): 152–160.

196 Cliff White, personal communication with author, 2016.

197 Cliff White, personal communication with author, 2016. See Robin Steenweg et al., "Assessing Potential Habitat and Carrying Capacity for Reintroduction of Plains Bison (*Bison bison bison*) in Banff National Park," *PLoS ONE* 11, no. 2 (2016), doi:10.1371/journal. pone.0150065.

198 Rob Jennings, personal communication with author, 2016.

199 Rick Smith, oral history, Park Warden Service Alumni Society, 2016.

200 Rob Jennings, oral history, Park Warden Service Alumni Society, 2016.

201 Rick Smith, oral history, Park Warden Service Alumni Society, 2016.

202 Marie Nylund, personal communication with author, 2016.

203 Jean Smith, oral history, Park Warden Service Alumni Society, 2016.

204 Rick Smith, oral history, Park Warden Service Alumni Society, 2016.

RMB | Rocky Mountain Books Ltd.
rmbooks.com
@rmbooks
facebook.com/rmbooks

Cataloguing data available from Library and Archives Canada
ISBN 9781771602280 (hardcover)
ISBN 9781771602297 (electronic)

Cover photo taken by Bradford White with evening light

Printed and bound in Canada by Friesens

Distributed in Canada by Heritage Group Distribution and in the U.S. by Publishers Group West

For information on purchasing bulk quantities of this book, or to obtain media excerpts or invite the author to speak at an event, please visit rmbooks.com and select the "Contact Us" tab.

RMB | Rocky Mountain Books is dedicated to the environment and committed to reducing the destruction of old-growth forests. Our books are produced with respect for the future and consideration for the past.

We acknowledge the financial support of the Government of Canada through the Canada Book Fund and the Canada Council for the Arts, and of the province of British Columbia through the British Columbia Arts Council and the Book Publishing Tax Credit.

KATHY CALVERT grew up in the Canadian Rockies. In 1974 she became one of the first female national park wardens in Canada; in 1977 she was a member of the first all-women expedition to Mount Logan; and in 1989 she was on the first all-women ski traverse of the Columbia Mountains from the Bugaboos to Rogers Pass. She is the author of three earlier books: *Don Forest: Quest for the Summits*, *Guardians of the Peaks: Mountain Rescue in the Canadian Rockies and Columbia Mountains* and *June Mickle: One Woman's Life in the Foothills and Mountains of Western Canada*. Kathy and her husband, Dale Portman, live in Cochrane, Alberta.